I REMEMBER

REVISITING
THE
LINDBERGH KIDNAPPING

Kevin Husted, Sr.

Absolute Author Publishing House
New Orleans, LA

Absolute Author
Publishing House

I Remember: Revisiting the Lindbergh Kidnapping
Copyright © 2019 Kevin Husted, Sr.

Publisher: Absolute Author Publishing House
Editor: Dr. Melissa Caudle
Line Editor: Kathy Rabb Kittok
Copy Editor: Tymothy Burke
Forward: Kevin Husted, Sr.
Cover Designer: Rebecca @Rebbecacovers
Photographs: From the United States Library of Congress in Public Domain (Library of Congress, Prints and Photographs Division, NYWT&S Collection,) under fair use policy or from the private collection of Kevin Husted, Sr.

LIBRARY OF CONGRESS IN-PUBLICATION-DATA

*I Remember: Revisiting the Lindbergh Kidnapping/*Kevin Husted Sr.

     p. cm.

Kevin Husted, Sr../ *I Remember: Revisiting the Lindbergh Kidnapping*

ISBN: 978-1-951028-26-8

1. Memoir   2. Autobiography   3. Historical Nonfiction

PRINTED IN THE UNITED STATES OF AMERICA

TABLE OF CONTENTS

I REMEMBER

KEVIN HUSTED, SR.

EDITORIAL NOTE

The contents of this book are personal in nature taken from the memoirs and an unpublished book drafted by Charles A. Lindbergh, Jr., now deceased, that he wrote before his death and now released by his son, the author and copyright owner.

It is not meant to be a historical record or account of the events; instead, it is the words taken from Charles A. Lindbergh, Jr. as he remembered and recorded them. There are gaps in the historical events due to the fact that Charles did not record them. This is the story that he always wanted the world to know and is a compilation of the notes, memoirs, and other documentation from Charles A. Lindbergh Jr. Although an effort was made to present Charles' story in chronological order, the names, places, etc., do not always appear in sequence due to the nature of the source material. Keeping this in mind, many names, dates, etc., while initially confusing, will become clear as you progress through the book.

The material for this book has been modified to the extent that duplications were removed from his journal or diary entries to enhance its readability. The punctuation and spelling have been corrected; however, the material has neither been rewritten nor censored.

Sample of Charles A. Lindbergh, Jr.'s Journal entry that I deciphered.

KEVIN HUSTED, SR.

Like most people upon hearing someone claim that they are the kidnapped son of Charles A. Lindbergh Sr. and Anne Morrow Lindbergh would be suspicious, I was too. I did my due diligence as a researcher with a Ph.D. in preparing the material for publication, I read and reread the contents a dozen times over. What struck me the most was Charles A. Lindbergh Jr.'s account of his childhood and how certain things aligned in his adulthood without question.

I reviewed hundreds of pages of documents, legal documents, newspaper articles, photos of the Lindbergh family and children, and historical records regarding the Lindbergh baby kidnapping and the investigation. I reviewed police records and the evidence associated with the crime, which led to the conviction of a man that pled his innocence up to the moment he was executed although he was offered a life sentence if he confessed.

FBI Washington DC 1930 Crime Lab - Photo courtesy of the Federal Bureau of Investigation

I REMEMBER

What I discovered was replete with inconsistencies, such as the size of the infant's body identified that was found in the woods that both Lindbergh Sr. and Betty Gow, the nurse, identified was severely decomposed and dismembered. How is positive identification of Lindbergh's son likely in such a case?

Additionally, the body discovered had a one-inch soft spot on the skull. The Lindbergh baby was twenty months old at the time, and according to medical authorities, a child of this age would not have one. Also, the baby was smaller by several inches than the Lindbergh baby. The only visible clue was the infant's clothes that both Lindbergh Sr. and Gow identified, which could have been exchanged by the kidnappers.

To add to the complication, the autopsy on the infant's body that was conducted comes into question; it was completed by a coroner who was not a physician, and then the body was quickly cremated leaving no forensic evidence.

There are myriad theories that state that the Lindbergh baby was either switched with a very sickly child and the mother was paid to do so or that the kidnappers and those involved dug up an infant's corpse and planted it to be found. Is it possible that both are true, and there was a payoff to many families to cover up the identity of the Lindbergh baby?

Charles A. Lindbergh Jr. has repeatedly requested for DNA analysis for his positive identification, but the Lindbergh family denied him and dismissed his claims. All of this could be answered with DNA analysis. In fact, there is a lock of Charles A. Lindbergh Jr.'s hair in a museum that could be used, but no one will agree to have it done.

One of the few pictures of Charles A. Lindbergh, Jr., as a child.

I REMEMBER

I may suggest that his story is believable in every account. You know the saying, "A picture is worth a thousand words," Charles A. Lindbergh Jr. carried a manila envelope filled with pictures of him and members of the Lindbergh family. The similarities are uncanny as he has the Lindbergh distinctive mouth, chin, broad nose, and hairline. Unfortunately, there are few pictures of Charles A. Lindbergh, Jr., growing up in his son's possession. According to his son, Kevin Husted, Sr., his father always believed it was because he couldn't be seen as he was under constant surveillance and movement between the Sigman's and Husted's households. If you search the internet, you will find maybe one or two of "Lucky Lindy" holding his son.

In 2003, he had a glimmer of hope that he might get an audience with the Lindbergh family when one woman, Astrid Bouteuil, and her two brothers, Dyrk and David Hesshaimer from Germany, came forward presenting DNA evidence from old love letters written by Charles A. Lindbergh Sr. to their mother, Brigitte Hesshaimer, a hat-maker, which stated he was their biological father. According to media consultant for the German children, "They knew all along he was their father." Additionally, they only knew him as Mr. Careu Kent.

After "Lucky Lindy's" death, his last will and testament revealed that he left part of his estate to the German family, thrusting the remaining siblings to accept them. Charles A. Lindbergh, Jr., has not been received with the same grace and understanding, but after editing this book and researching it, I think they should give him an audience and put this to rest once and for all. By doing so, one of two things will be proven; either the DNA will prove the Lindbergh baby's identity is Charles A. Lindbergh, Jr., or it will disprove it.

In 1997, Charles A. Lindbergh, Jr. underwent a polygraph test at his request. The polygraph examiner, Stanley L. Otremba, Ph.D., considered an expert with a distinguished resume, concluded that Charles was not deceptive in any of his answers, and held the professional opinion that Charles A. Lindbergh, Jr., was the son of the famous aviator as evidenced by the following documents. On the following pages.

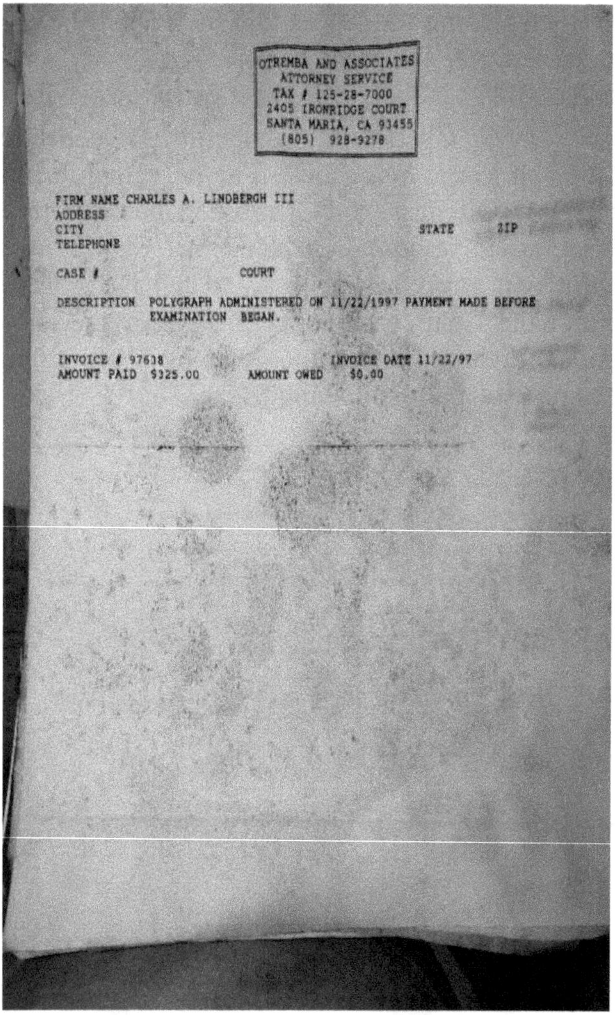

OTREMBA AND ASSOCIATES
ATTORNEY SERVICE
TAX # 125-28-7000
2405 IRONRIDGE COURT
SANTA MARIA, CA 93455
(805) 928-9278

FIRM NAME CHARLES A. LINDBERGH III
ADDRESS
CITY STATE ZIP
TELEPHONE

CASE # COURT

DESCRIPTION POLYGRAPH ADMINISTERED ON 11/22/1997 PAYMENT MADE BEFORE EXAMINATION BEGAN.

INVOICE # 97638 INVOICE DATE 11/22/97
AMOUNT PAID $325.00 AMOUNT OWED $0.00

Receipt of payment for the polygraph test.

KEVIN HUSTED, SR.

Copy of Original Polygraph Results. Note: The original paper is moldy and has smoke damage from a fire.

ANS: YES
DID YOU MAKE UP AND SCHEME ABOUT BEING THE KIDNAPPED SON
OF CHARLES AND ANNA LINDBERGH ON MARCH 1932?
ANS: NO

A TOTAL OF THREE (3) CHART EXAMINATIONS WERE CONDUCTED,
AND UPON REVIEWING AND SCORING THE TESTS IT IS THE OPINION
OF THIS EXAMINER THAT EXAMINE CHARLES LINDBERGH III,
SHOWED NO DECEPTION IN ALL RELEVANT QUESTIONS ASKED ON
THE EXAMINATION, AND IT IS THE OPINION AND BELIEF BY THIS
EXAMINER THAT MR. LINDBERGH, IS THE SON WHO WAS KIDNAPPED
IN MARCH OF 1932, AS STATED BEFORE ALL RELEVANT QUESTIONS
SHOWED NO DECEPTION.

SUBMITTED
STAN OTREMBA PhD
POLYGRAPH EXAMINER

Copy of Page 2 of Polygraph Results. Note: The original paper is moldy and has smoke damage from a fire.

KEVIN HUSTED, SR.

STANLEY L. OTREMBA PH.D.

PROFESSIONAL HIGHLIGHTS

SANTA BARBARA SHERIFF DETECTIVE IN CHARGE OF THE JUVENILE BUREAU, MAJOR CRIMES DETAIL

ASSISTANT STATION COMMANDER LOMPOC SUB-STATION 1970 -1972

STATION COMMANDER LOMPOC SUB-STATION 1972-1973.
ASSOCIATED INSTRUCTOR AT CHAPMAN AND LAVERNNE UNIVERSITY ASSOCIATED FACULTY MEMBER OF GOLDEN GATE UNIVERSITY, INSTRUCTOR IN THE GRADUATE MPA PROGRAM.

ALLAN HANCOCK COLLEGE FULL TENURED INSTRUCTOR IN THE ADMINISTRATION OF JUSTICE COURSES 1969 TO PRESENT

COORDINATOR OF THE SHERIFF RESERVE PROGRAM IN LOMPOC, AND ITS SEARCH AND RESCUE DETAIL.

GUEST LECTURER AT THE UNIVERSITY OF WARSAW POLAND.

PROGRESSIVE PUBLIC SERVICE RECORD

1965 -1983	PATROL DEPUTY SHERIFF. PROMOTED TO DETECTIVE. SERVICE IN THE JUVENILE BUREAU, MAJOR CRIME BUREAU, BURGLARY DETAIL.
1959-1965	DEPUTY SHERIFF LOS ANGELES COUNTY - PRIMARILY CIVIL DIVISION SUPERIOR COURT BAILIFF AND TRANSPORTATION DETAIL.
1955-1959	US NAVY. ASSIGNED TO THE AIR NAVAL INTELLIGENCE DIVISION. ASSISTANT TO THE INTELLIGENCE BRIEFING OFFICER IN TOP SECRET AND CONFIDENTIAL MATTERS.

PROFESSIONAL AFFILIATIONS AND PUBLICATIONS.

COPYRIGHT PUBLICATION OF Ph.D. DISSERTATION " MARITAL HARMONY AND STABILITY AS MEASURED BY PERSONALITY AND MOTIVATION IN LAW ENFORCEMENT MARRIAGES" 1980 UNITED STATES INTERNATIONAL UNIVERSITY

MEMBER OF THE ARSON -FIRE INVESTIGATORS ASSOCIATION.
MEMBER OF THE TRI/COUNTY INVESTIGATORS ASSOCIATION.

FORMAL ACADEMIC QUALIFICATIONS

JUNE 1980 PH.D. DEGREE AWARDED FROM UNITED STATES INTERNATIONAL UNIVERSITY.
JUNE 1973 MA DEGREE AWARDED FROM CHAPMAN COLLEGE. MAJOR IN EDUCATION.
JUNE 1971 BA DEGREE AWARDED FROM LA VERNE UNIVERSITY MAJOR ADMINISTRATION OF JUSTICE
JUNE 1969 AS DEGREE AWARDED FROM ALLAN HANCOCK COLLEGE. ADMINISTRATION OF JUSTICE
JUNE 1970 AA DEGREE AWARDED FROM ALLAN HANCOCK COLLEGE. SOCIOLOGY

Resume of Polygraph Examiner Page 1

PROFESSIONAL SCHOOLS/ SEMINARS

BASIC/ INTERMIATE / ADVANCE CERTIFICATES FROM P.O.S.T.
OFFICER SURVIVAL /TERRORISM/ SEX CRIMES CALIFORNIA STATE TRAINING INSTITUTE ARSON
INVESTIGATION FBI SEMINAR.
DRUG ABUSE /INVESTIGATIONS US DEPARTMENT OF DRUG ENFORCEMENT.
6 FBI SEMINARS DEALING WITH LAW ENFORCEMENT SPECIAL PROBLEMS
POLYGRAPH SCHOOL -1984 GORMAC / PAST APA MEMBER. LICENSED AS POLYGRAPH
EXAMINER BY STATE OF CALIFORNIA 1984.
100 HOURS OF SEMINAR INSTRUCTION ON REVIEW AND UPDATE IN POLYGRAPH
EXAMINATIONS AND INTERPRETATION
PRIVATE INVESTIGATOR LICENSE FROM STATE OF CALIFORNIA FROM 1984

PERSONAL STATISTICS

BORN ON SEPTEMBER 17, 1937
HEIGHT: 5'10"
WEIGHT: 195
MARRIED WITH ON DAUGHTER AND ONE SON. THEIR AGES 21 & 20 RESPECTIVELY. MY
HEALTH AND THAT OF MY FAMILY ARE GOOD.

> STANLEY L. OTREMBA
> 2405 IRONRIDGE COURT
> SANTA MARIA, CA 93455
> HOME: 805 928 9278
> OFFICE 922-6966 EXT 3250

Resume of Polygraph Examiner Page 2

KEVIN HUSTED, SR.

In December 1977, Charles wrote a letter to, "To Whom It May Concern," hoping that the world would recognize the polygraph results.

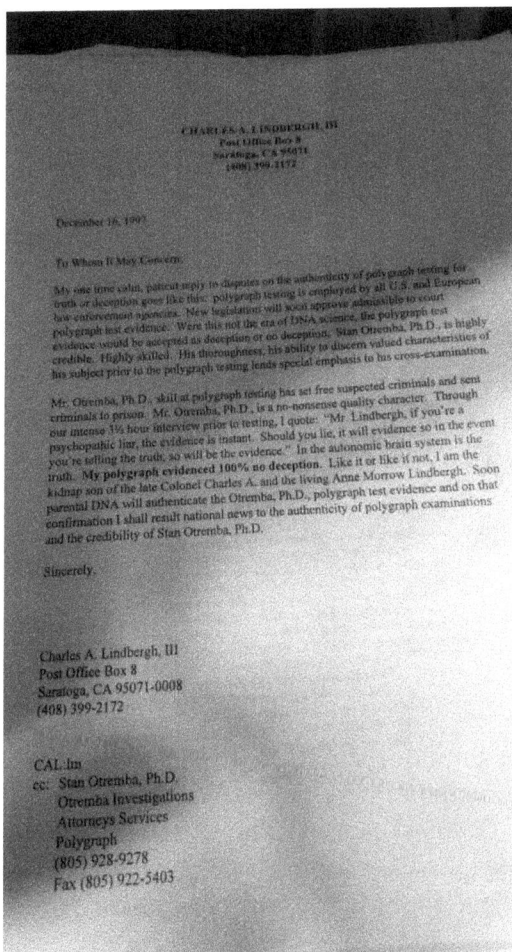

Copy of the original letter Charles A. Lindbergh, Jr., released.

He also authorized Dr. Otremba to disclose the polygraph findings to several individuals including respected news journalist Barbara Walters and the Lindbergh siblings, John, Land, Scott, and Reeve. He had nothing to hide.

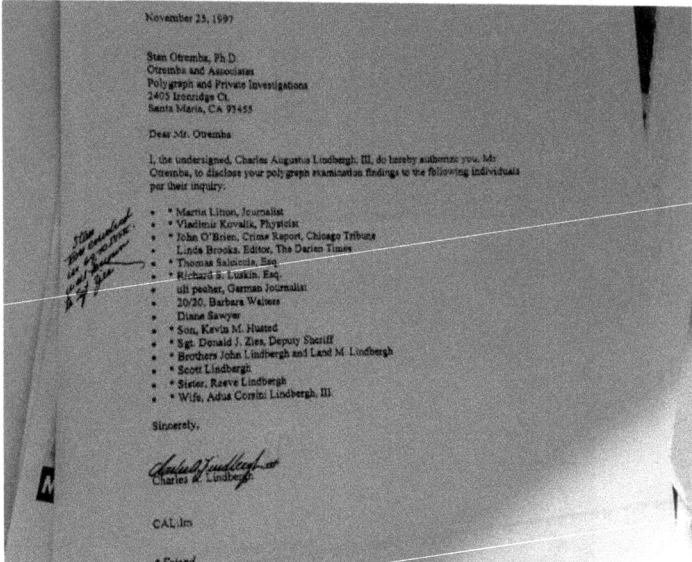

The letter written to release records along with Charles A. Lindbergh III's signature. He later changed his name to Jr., at the end of it.

One thing for sure is that Charles A. Lindbergh, Jr. led an extraordinary life filled with complications, hushed family secrets, deception, and misfortunes. There are things that he wrote that no one could have possibly known unless he or she was there at the moment. He recounts names, dates, and places that can make naysayers think twice.

I believe the honesty in his writing prevails, although it is at times painful to comprehend and absorb. Something went wrong somewhere in history, and it is evident in this book that his journey was painful. Somehow, I hope that he may now find peace in the afterlife because he finally got to tell his story.

Some may question the authenticity of this book; however, I believe he believed he was the son of Charles A. Lindbergh, Sr. The preponderance of the contents and his memories are daunting. Without the benefit of me ever meeting him, I feel I got to know his soul by editing his words. The question remains, will you and the rest of the world recognize him as the son of Charles A. Lindbergh, Sr. after reading his memoir? I'll leave that up to you and see if history must be rewritten.

Respectfully,
Dr. Melissa Caudle, Editor
Absolute Author Publishing House

Charles A. Lindbergh, Jr., kept many old newspaper articles about him and his father over the years.

FORWARD
BY KEVIN HUSTED, SR.

I am Kevin Husted, Sr., the biological son of Charles Augustus Lindbergh, Jr. Yes, that is my father's name, and he believes that he is the biological son of Charles A. Lindbergh, Sr., the famous aviator known to the world as "Lucky Lindy."

There are many conspiracies that have been put forth over the years regarding the kidnapping and death of the Lindbergh baby in 1932 -- the crime of the century which includes that Bruno Richard Hauptmann was tried, convicted, and executed for the murder. Some of the most damning evidence was a piece of lumber from a broken ladder which authorities believe came from his home and his spending several of the gold money certificates from the ransom money.

Yet, my father lived an extraordinary life, married, and had children, always believing that he was the Lindbergh baby up until his death. How can this possibly be true?

The Husted Family: Seated left to right – Brad, Charles A. Lindbergh, Jr., Kevin, and Kaye

Like most conspiracy theories concerning the Lindbergh baby kidnapping, there is a solid basis of facts that coincide, which for the most part, make them believable. Several of the arguments highlight Hauptmann as a scapegoat for a cover-up by Lindbergh, Sr. regarding the kidnapping of his son. Could such a man, held in high esteem worldwide, do such a thing to his son? That is for you to determine after my father outlines the facts of his life.

My father always believed that because of his physical deformity, his right club foot, Lindbergh, Sr., was embarrassed and wanted to hide the fact, so he masterminded the kidnapping plan. If that is true, the plan worked as a manhunt ensued with Lindbergh, Sr. at the helm. Weeks later, an infant's body was located near the Lindbergh's home. The only problem was that the body was badly decomposed and dismembered. There was no way to accurately identify that the infant discovered was the Lindbergh baby.

My father believed, that the infant who was discovered, wasn't the Lindbergh baby -- in essence it was another baby's body used to fake the death of the aviator's son.

After reading my father's words, you can determine for yourself if he was the son of Charles A. Lindbergh, Sr. His hope was always to paint a mosaic and provide a missing link to history, and possibly solve one of the greatest mysteries of all time.

He kept a diary and years later while undergoing regression hypnosis, he recalled many events, and Charles and Anne Morrow Lindbergh whom he believed were his biological parents.

In fact, he accurately recalled many details that no one could have known unless they were there, one of which was him meeting Al Capone's sister long before anyone knew of her existence. How can that be unless he actually met her?

I'm not asking anyone to believe my father's life-story because my father believed or that as his son, I believe it. I'm only asking that you read this book with an open mind, clarity, and without judgment to discover the truth.

In offering some proof, I present several government documents – his birth certificate, driver's license, his social security card, and his Medicaid insurance card.

I REMEMBER

Copy of the original Birth Certificate my father carried in his wallet until the day he died. He kept it wrapped in a piece of foil.

KEVIN HUSTED, SR.

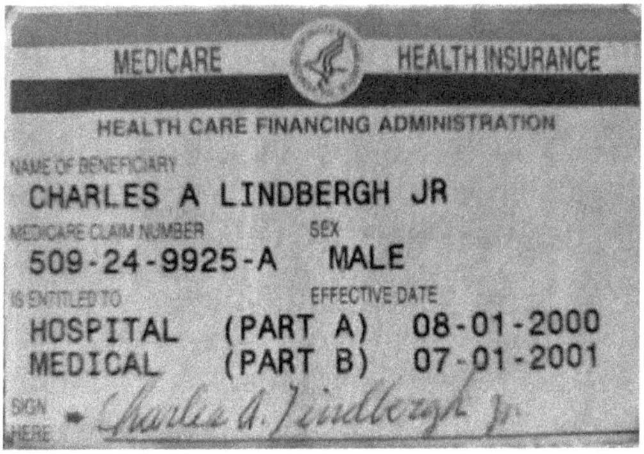

I REMEMBER

How is it that my father's birthday, June 22, 1930, is the same date as Lindbergh's baby, and their names are identical? Do you suppose that is a coincidence? No, my father was given that name at birth, and that is what is on his birth certificate and his death certificate.

My question to you, the reader is, "If the government recognizes my dad as Charles A. Lindbergh Jr., and his birthday is June 22, 1930, why can't the rest of the world accept this?" They are the United States government, after all.

Instead, my dad fought his entire life to prove his true identity, including contacting the Lindbergh family. He openly asked for DNA analysis but was denied by them. Why refuse a DNA paternity test if there isn't something to hide? What would the Lindbergh family have to lose, except billions of dollars?

In an interview, my Dad said, "I contacted my sister Reeve, and she said that they don't know me, they didn't grow up with me, and they owe me nothing."

Don't you think the Lindbergh family could solve this mystery once and for all by agreeing to a DNA test on my father? But, they won't, which makes me even more curious to know why and question what they could possibly be hiding? Could they be protecting Charles A. Lindbergh, Sr., and his involvement with the crime of the century to protect the Colonel's legacy? If not, then why not agree to the DNA analysis?

In 1998, a close friend of my family, Wayne Sparks, who was also a bodyguard for my dad; Lindbergh, Jr. for twenty-two years, interceded on my father's behalf in trying to obtain a DNA sample and have the family cooperate in obtaining positive identification. They traveled to Connecticut to meet with Anne Morrow Lindbergh and went to her house. They walked up to the driveway and saw her, and another lady believed to be taking care of her getting into a car. The lady screamed, "Your sister said you cannot see your mother, acknowledging that Charles was, in fact, Lindbergh's son."

Sparks had a camera that day and tried to take pictures and videos, but Anne attempted to take the camera away. Charles intervened and said, "You're not taking this camera away."

Charles had brought a bouquet to give to his mother that day but was unable to do so. Later that day, they went back to Winchester, where they were staying, and my dad called the police department. According to Sparks, the police told them, "That if you go back to that house again, we'll arrest you. The best thing for you to do is to get out of town."

On another note, Reeve Lindbergh stated that her father had three other relationships in Europe outside of his marriage with her mother resulting seven children, and she hadn't heard of them until 2003 when one of the women, Astrid, broke her silence and said, "I can't do this anymore."

Reeve Lindbergh initially thought Astrid and her brothers were either crazy or lying, but ultimately recognized the illegitimate children, but never my father. The convincing factor was when one of Reeve's nephews went to Europe and met Astrid and her brothers and initiated a DNA test which proved they were in fact a Lindbergh.

After "Lucky Lindy" died, Reeve discovered that her father had left a portion of his wealth in three separate trust funds for those other siblings. Reeve made a poignant statement during a presentation on May 10, 2008, at the Wisdom House in Connecticut when she spoke about her mother to one of her mother's closest friends. Reeve asked her, "If my mother knew." In Reeve's own words, she recalled her mother's friend saying, "I think she knew; I don't think she knew what she knew; she knew something. And the other thing she said was that she thought it had to do with the child, the lost baby who died. Never in my whole life, I never heard him talk about that child."

"That child," referring to my dad was heartbreaking for my father. To me, there is something unnerving about Reeve's statement because Lindbergh, Sr., was so involved with the investigation and search for his son; yet, he didn't talk about him to his other children. Why? I can only speculate. It could be the pain of losing a child or guilt.

On countless occasions, with his attorney, my father contacted the FBI and several members of Congress to get help in proving his identity including asking for help from Congressman Mike Honda and Senator Diane Feinstein.

KEVIN HUSTED, SR.

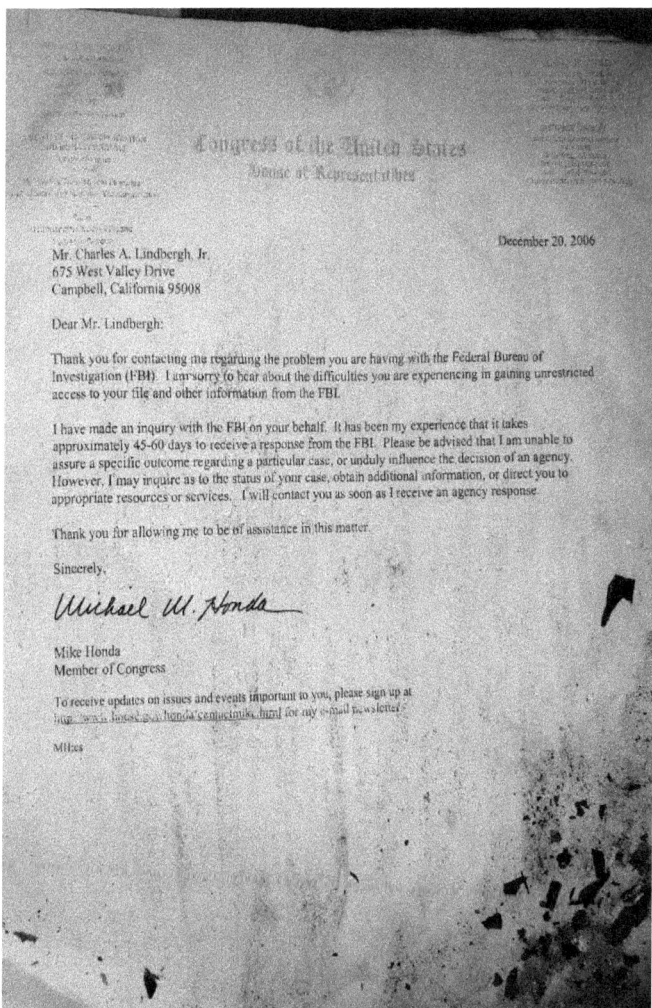

Copy of Letter to Congressman Honda

I REMEMBER

Senator Dianne Feinstein

Privacy Release Form

Complete, sign, and return to:
SENATOR DIANNE FEINSTEIN
ONE POST STREET, SUITE 2450
SAN FRANCISCO, CA 94104

Date: November 11, 2006

Name: CHARLES A. LINDBERGH III

Address: 675 WEST VALLEY DR. CAMPBELL, CALIFORNIA   Zip: 95008

Home Phone: 408 369 9488

Work Phone: 408 369 9488

Federal Agency Involved: FBI

Social Security # or Agency File #: 509 24 9925

Have you contacted our office before? NO

Have you contacted another congressional office regarding this matter? YES
If "yes" to the above, which office & when? REP. MICHAEL HONDA 10/31/2006

Is this matter currently pending before a local, state, or federal court? NO

Problem:
Please briefly explain your problem and outline the steps that have been taken by you and the agency with regards to your situation. In addition, please make your request for assistance as specific as possible. Should you require more room, feel free to attach a letter addressed directly to the Senator.

There has been prolonged, systematic and unexplained harassment and defamation by the FBI affecting my health and business career over a period of many years. The FBI has kept a secret file on me for those many years, even though I have no history of criminal activity.

My attorney requested the FBI file under the FOIA Act, but they refused delivery of most of the file claiming that releasing it would invade the privacy of others (whom they did not identify)

Copy of the document for release of records from FBI to Senator Dianne Feinstein

My father reached out countless times to the Lindbergh siblings, his mother, and father, as did Adua Corsini Lindbergh, his fourth wife. On one occasion, my stepmother received a response from Reeve Lindbergh.

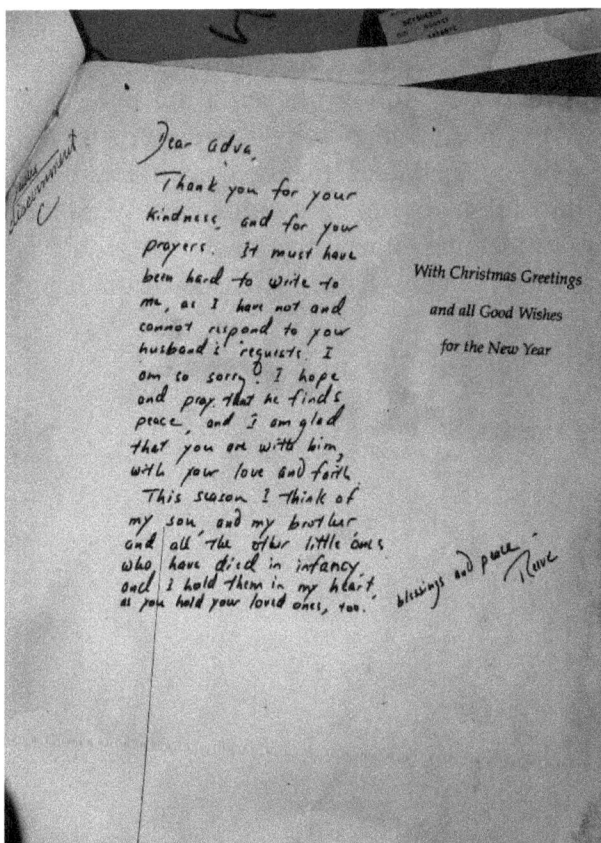

Copy of letter received from Reeve Lindbergh

I REMEMBER

My father died before he could publish his book, but he dreamed that someone, someday would come forth and do the right thing and tell the whole story. He always wanted the world to know that he was alive and for everyone to understand what happened to him. Instead, he went to his grave, rejected by the Lindbergh family, and denied being a part of the family.

Out of respect for my father, I am publishing his story. My father neither sought fame nor fortune and only wanted for all concerned to come forward and tell the truth and give testimony to his identity. Somebody knows something other than my father. This is my father's story, and his name is Charles A. Lindbergh Jr.

Respectfully,

Kevin Husted, Sr.

KEVIN HUSTED, SR.

THE LINDBERGH BABY KIDNAPPING REVISITED

Charles Augustus Lindbergh, Jr., the twenty-month-old son of the famous aviator Charles A. Lindbergh, Sr., and Anne Morrow Lindbergh, was kidnapped between 9:00 – 9:30 p.m., on March 1, 1932, from the second-floor nursery of the Lindbergh's home. Betty Gow, the child's nurse, discovered that the baby was missing around 10:00 p.m. when she went to check on him. She reported to the police that she put the baby to bed at 7:30 p.m.

After reporting him missing to Charles Lindbergh, Sr., who was downstairs in his library, a search by him, with the help of his butler, Olly Whateley, ensued and a ransom note demanding $50,000 was isolated on the nursery windowsill.

Whateley immediately called the Hopewell Borough Police Department, and Lindbergh immediately contacted his attorney, Henry Breckinridge, who was

1

also one of his friends, and it is alleged that he also contacted the New Jersey State Police who ultimately had jurisdiction over the investigation.

According to the police records, during the search at the crime scene, the baby's blanket, mud traces, two different sets of footprints, and pieces of a wooden ladder were found beneath the nursery window. One odd thing struck the investigators – one of the two sections of the ladder had split, which indicated that the ladder had been broken, and it was surmised this most likely during the kidnapping.

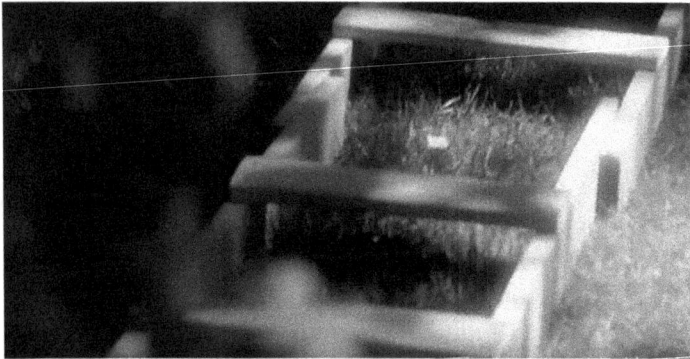

Reproduction of Ladder

Another finding was that there was no evidence of blood in or around the nursery, and zero evidence of fingerprints except for the baby's, which meant whoever kidnapped the infant was extremely careful to cover their tracks.

The ransom note that Lindbergh found was replete with errors, both spelling and grammatical, and later a handwriting expert said that the author of the note was likely a German immigrant. The note, as written, said:

KEVIN HUSTED, SR.

Dear Sir!
Have 50.000$ redy 25 000$ in
20$ bills 15000$ in 10$ bills and
10000$ in 5$ bills After 2–4 days
we will inform you were to deliver
the mony.

We warn you for making
anyding public or for notify the Police
The child is in gut care.
Indication for all letters are
Singnature
and 3 hohls

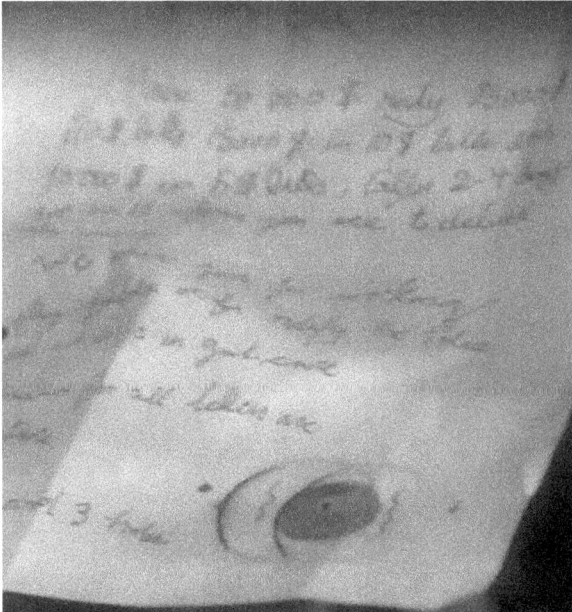

Recreation of Kidnapper Note

I REMEMBER

Because word of the kidnapping quickly spread, hundreds of people flocked to the crime scene, which destroyed any chance of obtaining evidence from the footprints. An expert, in the first known case to use forensic evidence, was called in who analyzed the handwriting and the wood of the ladder.

The morning after the kidnapping, President Herbert Hoover was notified and immediately arranged for the Department of Justice to intervene in the investigation. During this time, kidnapping was a state crime and not federal; therefore, this was not an ordinary procedure. However, because it was a high-profile case, President Hoover thought it best.

Distraught over the kidnapping, Colonel Lindbergh asked his influential friends to intervene and to make widespread appeals to contact the kidnappers.

He left no stone unturned, including using known mobsters such as Mickey Rosner, Al Capone, Willie Moretti, and Abner Zwellman. Mrs. Lindbergh even published the baby's diet hoping that the kidnappers would take care of her son until he was returned.

KEVIN HUSTED, SR.

WANTED

INFORMATION AS TO THE WHEREABOUTS OF

CHAS. A. LINDBERGH, JR.

OF HOPEWELL, N. J.

SON OF COL. CHAS. A. LINDBERGH

World-Famous Aviator

This child was kidnaped from his home in Hopewell, N. J., between 8 and 10 p. m. on Tuesday, March 1, 1932.

DESCRIPTION:

Age, 20 months   Hair, blond, curly
Weight, 27 to 30 lbs.   Eyes, dark blue
Height, 29 inches   Complexion, light
Deep dimple in center of chin
Dressed in one-piece coverall night suit

ADDRESS ALL COMMUNICATIONS TO
COL. H. N. SCHWARZKOPF, TRENTON, N. J., or
COL. CHAS. A. LINDBERGH, HOPEWELL, N. J.

ALL COMMUNICATIONS WILL BE TREATED IN CONFIDENCE

COL. H. NORMAN SCHWARZKOPF
March 11, 1932   Supt. New Jersey State Police, Trenton, N. J.

A second note was found, and then on March 8, 1932, the third ransom note was received by Breckinridge stating that the kidnappers would not accept an intermediary and that Lindbergh must place a note in the newspaper to make contact.

That same day, a retired school principal, Dr. John F. Condon, published an offer to act as the go-between and offered $1,000 on top of the ransom demand. The next day, another ransom note was received by Dr. Condon informing him he was an acceptable go-between. Colonel Lindbergh provided Dr. Condon with the $70,000 in cash, and as a result, the retired principal started negotiations for payment using a newspaper column under the code name, "Jafsie."

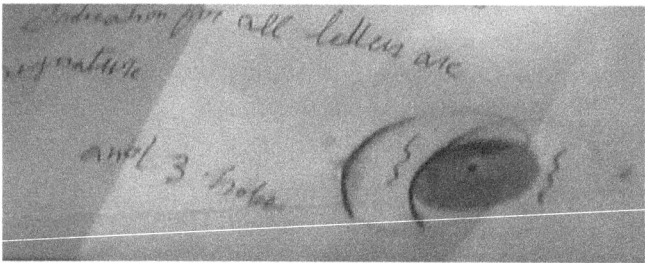

Signature of the Kidnapper - Recreation

On the evening of March 12, 1932, around 8:30 p.m., Dr. Condon received a note delivered by Joshep Perrone, a taxicab driver. He could not identify the man who handed him the note. This note was not a ransom note but contained the message where the next ransom note would be located, one hundred feet from a subway station.

Once that note was obtained, Dr. Condon followed the directions and met with an unidentified man, "John," at Woodlawn Cemetery where they discussed payment of the ransom. It was during this meeting that "John" agreed to provide proof that he had the baby, which ultimately came in the mail along with another ransom note. To prove the baby's identity, the kidnapper sent one of the baby's nightgowns to Dr. Condon on March 16, 1932, which was verified by Charles Lindbergh that it once belonged to his son.

As promised, Condon continued to place advertisements in the newspaper, and on March 21, 1932, another ransom note was received by him stating that compliance was necessary. The note also suggested that the kidnapping had been planned for a year.

Days passed as the Lindbergh's continued their search. Finally, on March 29, 1932, the nurse, Betty Gow, located the baby's thumb guard at the entrance of the Lindbergh estate.

Another ransom note was received by Dr. Condon on March 30, 1932, whereby the kidnappers threatened to increase the ransom to $100,000. They also refused to use the code in the newspaper columns.

Then on April 1, 1932, Dr. Condon received a further ransom demand instructing him to have the money ready by the next night. To acknowledge compliance, Dr. Condon placed another ad in the paper. An unidentified taxi driver later delivered another note, and Dr. Condon found the twelfth ransom note under a stone, located at 3225 East Tremont Avenue, Bronx, New York.

I REMEMBER

That same evening, Dr. Condon met with "John" again to reduce the demand to $50,000. He handed "John" the $50,000 cash and in exchange received another note specifying the location of the child. According to records, the Lindbergh baby would be found on a boat named *Nellie* docked near Martha's Vineyard in Massachusetts. The search the next day proved fruitless as the baby was not found and the authorities continued the search.

Years passed, and still no answers despite the numerous suspects in the pool. Then on May 12, 1932, about four and a half miles from the Lindbergh's estate, William Allen, an assistant on a truck, and the truck driver, Orville Wilson, pulled over to go to the restroom. They discovered an infant's body about forty-five feet from the highway in Mercer County.

The body was extremely decomposed, the head had been crushed, and the skull bore a hole. One fatal clue as to the identity of the baby was missing -- several body parts were removed, including the deformed foot of the Lindbergh baby.

The death certificate stated that the infant died from a blow to the head and the infant's body was immediately cremated leaving no chance for DNA evidence.

The Conspiracy Revisited

Many questions surfaced for me when I reviewed the details of the search. Imagine being me for a second. How could they have identified the infant who was found as the son of Charles Lindbergh? Umm, the deformed foot was missing, and the body was severely decomposed. Then, I must question how the truck drivers found the infant's body. Happenstance? I don't think so.

Also, of importance, Charles A. Lindbergh, Sr. was eminently involved in the search, throughout the investigation, and during the trial of the accused. I believe that was a conflict of interest. I'm not going to revisit the arrest, prosecution, or execution of the man convicted for the kidnapping because I believe he was a scapegoat, and information supporting my conclusion is easily located on the web.

From here on out, you will read my encounter from my journal and diaries as I remember the events of my life and why I think I am the son of Charles A. Lindbergh, Sr. I remember it all.

My Earliest Memories

THE SIGMAN FARMHOUSE

1934 to 1935 - Bunkhouse Kitchen of Charles Spencer "Charlie" Sigman and Wife Katie Sigman, Rural Route One, Butler County, Kansas, El Dorado, Kansas township

Time: It was after lunch.

Charles Augustus Lindbergh, Sr., and his wife Anne Morrow Lindbergh, whom I believe are my biological parents, landed at Wichita, Kansas airport. The time and date of their landing information were recorded in my father's flight logbook and my mother's 1934 - 1935 diary. They were loaned a green car to commence their search for me through the Rural Route 1 area of Butler County, Kansas, El Dorado, Kansas. The question is, "Who directed my parents to Rural Route 1, to the

Charles S. and Katie Mitchell Sigman farmhouse?" What made them want to come? Was it to see me?

Rural Route 1, Butler County

They arrived in the early afternoon; my parents turned off Rural Route 1 into the Sigman's farmhouse driveway that opened into a sizeable tar-covered truck yard. In an estimated twenty feet from the bunkhouse kitchen, if their curiosity pointed their attention to the vacant yellow tenant houses and shed past the saddle tack house on the far edge of the truck yard, to the right of the single garage was a brown on brown Hudson sport coupe. In those split seconds, had Anne, my mother, looked to the right, she would have seen me before I was whisked up the narrow stairs to the bunkhouse kitchen bedroom by Katie Sigman.

The afore-described scenes are not cryptomeria memory blooms. The scene described is as close to exactly the same as my memory stream and is generally void of being fabricated by my imagination or illusion.

11

I REMEMBER

In 1998, the Charles S. Sigman farmhouse and bunkhouse kitchen were restored and painted canary yellow with green trim as it was in 1935. My last visit there occurred in 1960. I have no pictures. When we visited the farmhouse, I felt confident about the accuracy of my memory stream.

When the bunkhouse kitchen phone rang, I was seated with my back to the cream color Kelvinator cooler and low sill window to the right of it. Charlie Sigman was washing up for lunch at the washbasin, which was to the left of the wall phone at the door entrance that led onto the causeway to the milk house. Katie Sigman was at the wood range, which was to the left of the washbasin.

The wall phone interested me as it began to ring. With a towel in his hand, Charlie picked up the receiver and acknowledged the caller from the Wichita, Kansas Airport. When listening to the caller, Charlie turned to view me with an expression of concern. Charlie covered the receiver with his hand and stated, "My God, Katie, Lindbergh has landed at Wichita. He's headed this way in a green car looking for his kid."

I remember those words as they still haunt me. I had already begun to wonder if I didn't belong with the Sigman's, and now I know why. I didn't belong to them. I belonged to Lindbergh, and I was his kid.

Charlie hung up the phone as Katie looked at me.

I had drunk a glass of milk and eaten Oreo cookies. I had a view of the car covered truck yard, the drive going out to the Rural Route 1 dirt road, and of the closed down roadhouse across the pasture where peanuts were cropped.

I rose from the table and moved to look out the low sill green trimmed window. My chin rested on the sill. I looked left and saw Katie taking a white porcelain milk pitcher from the table. Katie opened the Kelvinator door, and I watched her put the pitcher inside.

Charlie Sigman

It was at this point that my attention was drawn to a green car that stopped in the drive. With my chin and hands on the windowsill, I pushed up onto my toes. My heart pounded against my ribcage; a gleeful exhilaration throbbed. I could make no noise, like being speechless. I can remember the attractive lady seated in the passenger seat, and if asked, I can easily draw a composite of her. She was Anne Morrow Lindbergh. She is that etched in my memory. The driver, I am certain, was the famous aviator Charles A. Lindberg, Sr., and he had come to see me.

In a hushed tone, as he rose to his feet, Charlie told Katie, "My God, it's them. Get the kid up the stairs and keep him quiet."

I turned my head to follow Charlie when he exited the door. I could see him pass the causeway window as Katie whisked me away with her fat hand clasped over my mouth. She dragged me up the narrow steep stairs to the bunkhouse kitchen bedroom. With me grasped in her arms, Katie pulled down the green-black window blind and seated herself on the bed, clutching me on her lap. Still clasping my mouth with her fat hand, Charlie soon came up and said, "They're gone."

We sat a long time in the dark before I was taken by Katie from the bunkhouse to the dark parlor room in the family farmhouse. I was a noiseless child; the parlor, a room from which a child could not escape; so, I remained silent.

Several Days Later – Sometime in the Afternoon

The time of day was afternoon. Charlie and Katie were quietly talking. Katie was at the wood range and moved back and forth to the cabinet of condiments, a flour bin, and a glass butter churn sitting on the porcelain countertop. Charlie held me firm on his lap; he restrained my arms as I resisted, then with great force, he twisted and pinch-rolled my chin crushing my chin cleft. I shrieked and screamed from the pain. Of course, I was not aware of the reason for his abuse.

1934 to 1935 - Traveling to 241 South Volutsia Street, Wichita, Kansas from Rural Route One, El Dorado, Kansas – Predawn

It was early predawn, and it was dark outside when Charlie awakened me. He and Katie were already dressed, and soon, I too was dressed to travel.

The yard lights were on, and the house lights were out. I watched Charlie walking to the distant garage. Katie and I waited on the causeway boards near the overhead yard light. Soon Charlie pulled up in the brown on brown Hudson sport coupe. I was placed in the center of the seat between them. After a bit, I laid my head in Katie's lap and viewed with interest the dash lights and radio knobs. The radio was playing soft music. I soon dozed off; I'm sure I did.

THE HUSTED HOUSEHOLD

1934 to 1935 - 241 South Volutsia Street, Wichita, Kansas, the Residence of Loren McFadden Husted and Wife, Myrtle Husted

In my waking moments, I remember being wrapped in a blanket and carried by Charlie, from the driver side around the back of the Hudson and into the house belonging to Loren McFadden Husted. Now, as then, I can vividly see Katie ahead of us looking to the sky. I saw the profile of an elm tree to our right and a steep roof to our left, which was very impressive against the blue sky.

The porch was dark. There was a screen door. We were let in and took a seat to the left of the entrance. We sat in the dark well into early daylight, and I fell asleep. When I was awake, I was a silent child, a non-stirring child, until mid-morning that day when I was held tight for a haircut. I was held down for a scrub on the kitchen sink drainboard, then dried and dressed. Soon all my pent-up pressures since my kidnapping began to escalate into heated protests.

The Sigmans and the Husteds decided to name me Loren Paul Husted.

"No, no, no, no," I said, "That's not my name; you're not my family. I will kill you people. No, no, no, that's not my name!" I knew then, as I do now, that this was wrong. That wasn't my name. My name is Charles A. Lindbergh Jr. I remember.

Jumping up from his chair, Don Wesley Husted, Sr., ripped off his belt to beat me, but Charlie Sigman immediately got up and punched him in the face and wrestled him to the floor.

Myrtle Husted picked me up and took me out to the kitchen.

Later that morning, it could have been around noon, I lost myself in the alleyway going north and was found four hours later at the corner of Volutsia Street and English Street. To my knowledge and what I can remember, no one summoned the police when I disappeared.

Dorothy Husted found me and walked me back to the Loren and Myrtle Husted residence. When asked where I had been, I replied, "With a man in a black suit smoking a big pipe." I remember this like it was yesterday and can still smell the aroma of that man's pipe tobacco.

Husted, Sr., again angered at my arrogance, was assured by Charlie Sigman with a harsh warning. He said, "I'll kill you, Don, if you ever beat that kid."

1934 to 1935 - 241 South Volutsia Street, Wichita, Kansas Residence of Loren McFadden Husted, and Myrtle Husted – Days Later

A simple, quiet lady, observant and intuitive, Myrtle Husted paused in the hallway entrance to the front room where her husband, Loren Husted, sat with his son, Don W. Husted, Sr. I was near her backside. Myrtle turned, stroked my brow, and said to Loren, "There is something terribly wrong. This is not Paul. This boy has a cowlick. I'm calling the police." Why would she say that?

Loren Husted and Don Husted, Sr., went into a rage calling Myrtle stupid, dumb, crazy, a bitch, and threatened to have her committed to the Lampard, Kansas asylum for the insane. Myrtle, I am sure was stunned at these accusations.

In that time frame, Loren Husted and his wife Myrtle fitted me with Paul Parrott high-top leather corrective shoes to correct my right foot position from a critical pigeon toe to straight. At bedtime, Myrtle removed my corrective shoes.

Loren Husted would wrap my twisted toes on a fudgesicle stick bound with adhesive tape. The excruciating pain in my legs was a mental nightmare. Awakened by my cries, Loren and Myrtle, kind people, would rise at all hours of the night to rub alcohol on my legs.

1934 to 1935 - 241 South Volutsia Street, Wichita, Kansas, the Residence of Loren McFadden Husted, and Myrtle Husted – Days Later

Loren McFadden Husted and a Bob Downing were cronies for a long time. The two were federal postal mail clerks with the Rock Island RR Line traveling round trip from Wichita, Kansas, to Monet, Missouri. Are these scenes the result of my parents' visits to the Sigmans' farmhouse? Could it be the FBI Special agents were in the immediate area?

Were these scenes the result of Myrtle Husted's phone visit with the wife of Bob Downing?

Bob Downing had told Loren Husted that an FBI special agent, who was long-time acquaintance, had asked him to take me, now named Paul, to the FBI office. Loren was reluctant to do so and became hostile. Eventually, however, he agreed, and Loren Husted and Bob Downing took me to the office of the FBI in the Federal Building.

I can vividly picture the activity of this visit as we walked up the gray concrete steps to the Federal

Building. Loren Husted, Bob Downing, and I entered through the left door entrance. Loren seated me on the Masonite wall to wall counter with a top lift entrance opener on the left end. Bob Downing introduced Loren Husted, and the FBI special agent handed me his gold shield to toy with, and as the FBI special agent plucked me from the countertop, I could see Bob Downing passing through the far-right door, suitcase in hand. With his shield in my hand, the FBI special agent carried me around the office and to a second standing FBI special agent. Soon Loren Husted and I were on our way through the right door entrance. He took me to the basement of the Federal Postal dispatch office.

As a child, I didn't know what was happening or why I was in a very large office meeting these people.

1934 to 1935 - 241 South Volutsia Street, Wichita, Kansas, the Residence of Loren McFadden Husted and Wife, Myrtle Husted – Several Weeks Later – Mid-Morning

The time was mid-morning when several police officers and a well-dressed man entered 241 South Volutsia Street. These people were seated with Loren Husted and Don Wesley Husted, Sr., at the dining table near the hallway.

Myrtle Husted took me from this scene to the front room where she had been visiting with their friend Otto J. Klink, a dapper dressed German immigrant who had taken a serious interest in their daughter, Dorothy Husted. Klink was demonstrating an Electrolux rubber garment bag that he had blown up.

KEVIN HUSTED, SR.

I escaped from Myrtle long enough to view the police, Loren Husted, and Don Husted sorting through several baby pictures. Myrtle quickly brought me back to the front room and firmly sat me on a footstool. Soon the conversation between the police and the Husteds escalated into a heated argument and shouting match that ended with the police and the well-dressed man hurriedly leaving the premises.

Situations like these, you don't tend to forget.

THE FBI AND SURVEILLANCE

1934 to 1938 - FBI Surveillance Activity at 241 South Volutsia Street, Wichita, Kansas, the Residence of Loren McFadden Husted, and Myrtle Husted.

FBI surveillance began shortly after that. Loren and Myrtle argued often; Dorothy was extremely disturbed. Reverend Don Wesley Husted, Sr. and his wife, Viola, were rarely present. Loren Husted frequently phoned the police demanding an investigation. The police desk person(s) continuously said, "There is no need for concern." Each phone call resulted in the same reply.

Loren Husted hung his .38 caliber, Smith and Wesson, on the bedpost during the night, and on the desktop during the day. He harshly instructed me not to touch his revolver, ever. He also suffered many sleepless nights and would often stand to look through the window at a man in a shiny black automobile who was dressed in a dark suit, white shirt, and black tie.

During the day, another man similarly dressed would park in front or park a house away or across the street, and so on through the night. On one occasion, in the late afternoon, when I was riding my white with black trim Schwinn tricycle, a second man drove up behind the parked auto. He was wearing a gun and walked to visit the occupant of the long-time parked automobile. I remember the gun all too well as I had been told many times never to touch one.

He eventually drove away leaving behind the other man who re-entered the car and remained there through the evening.

In the summertime, the Husteds often gathered on the front lawn to visit, sip tea or lemonade, and enjoy Myrtle's homemade donuts and ice cream.

On my tricycle, I peddled to the character in the shiny black car and told him hello. This man looked at me and grinned. It seemed strange to me. What was he doing there?

Wichita, Kansas, FBI Surveillance Activity at 241 South Volutsia Street, Wichita, Kansas, the Residence of Loren McFadden Husted, and Myrtle Husted

Myrtle Husted and I were followed downtown by those men in the shiny black cars. We may have been followed many times, but I was unaware of it.

Myrtle shopped at Sears & Roebuck, Henry's, Carl's Shoe, Kress's, Woolworth 5/10, Landrum's Market and a bakery, a poultry house, a dairy, Ceros' Candy Kitchen, King's X Hamburgers, Ralph Baum Hamburger Stand, and English Street Grocery Store.

I REMEMBER

She walked swiftly; maybe it only seemed that way since I was a young child. I always remained quiet when shopping, and when we walked down the downtown streets, she always had a firm grasp of my hand. Myrtle was never careless with my life, for which I will always be eternally grateful.

On occasion, Myrtle complained to her husband, Loren, of being followed and felt that at times, she was followed when shopping at the stores, and I pondered why the frequent photography antics occurred when she was shopping downtown. I must admit it all seemed strange to me as a child, but I remember it extremely well.

During the summer and winter, Myrtle and I often had our pictures taken by one, sometimes two photographers with flash cameras.

Whoever these people were, they snapped pictures, and popped flashbulbs for blocks from the rear, the street side, kneeling, and snapping away only three feet to ten feet away and continuously moving ahead of us.

We would enter Woolworth 5/10, and on returning to the sidewalk, the photographers would be there. I remember one photographer telling the second photographer, "Get back to the office."

On another occasion, a photographer moved to the curb and entered a waiting auto after several blocks of camera flashes. As a child, I couldn't help but wonder what all the fuss was about and why were they taking my picture. Who were these people, and what did they want?

1939 – At 2101 South Oliver Street, Wichita, Kansas Residence of Loren McFadden Husted, and Myrtle Husted

Loren and Myrtle Husted moved into their new residence at 2101 South Oliver Street, Wichita, Kansas, a Klessen subdivision. I don't remember why we moved, only that we did.

Myrtle enrolled me at Hillside Country School, approximately four miles down Mt. Vernon Road to hillside road from Oliver Street.

Charles A. Lindbergh, Jr. playing on back of a truck in 1939.

BACK TO THE FARMHOUSE

1935 to 1944 - Rural Route 1, Butler County, Kansas, (El Dorado, Kansas). Farmhouse Residence of Charles S. "Charlie" Sigman and Rife, Katie Sigman

Cameron the Cowhand

Once I went to live with the Husteds, I still returned to see the Sigman's. I'm not certain as to why I taken, and I can only ascertain it was because the Husteds and Sigmans were friends.

Throughout the 1935 to 1944-time frame, I visited the Sigmans' homestead, which consisted of 1000 acres. An individual who I vividly remember was a tall cowhand named Cameron. He seemed too clean-cut for a farmhand, and he daily worked the twenty-two head of horses. He also frequently traveled into Wichita, Kansas, for unspecified reasons.

Charlie and Katie had their suspicions of Cameron, and they fired him for being absent too often. Cameron was always observant of me and played his impressions on Willie Louise Sigman to stay close.

Picture taken in 1939 - Left to right - C. G. Sigman, Willie Louise, unknown, and Charles A. Lindbergh Jr.

Howard Hull

The second person was Howard Hull, a test pilot for the Stearman Aircraft Company in Wichita, Kansas. He was the son of the owner of Hull Tire Service. Consequently, Stearman Aircraft built the C-36, the type of plane my dad, Charles A. Lindbergh, Sr. flew to survey air routes for Transcontinental and Western Airways.

Howard frequently dated Willie Louise up through her marriage to her cousin, Ralph Young. Howard often visited me, and the Husteds, on his Indian motorcycle. His observations were impressive. He had frequent communications with the FBI and was the source that tipped off Willie Louise of my being the Lindbergh boy.

Howard met with Charlie Sigman's violent temper, and one night, they had a terrible fistfight. I was scared to death. That night, Charlie threatened to kill Howard, but Howard remained calm, seeing that he could withstand lots of pressure being a successful test pilot.

As a result of Howard and Charlie's fight, Willie Louise learned about my identity and was told by Howard that I was the Lindbergh boy who was kidnapped. The news didn't settle with her very well, and she began to drink, take barbiturates, and frequently would get hysterical when I visited the farm.

Willie Louise

Her pleads to come clean with my identity enhanced my memory activity. She was scared and wanted to come clean, but no one would allow it. Willie Louise grew very ill. Fear of them going to prison and the violent threats from her father, Charlie Sigman, took a critical toll on her life. She grew obese and more hysterical every time I came around the house.

The frequent pleas made by Willie Louise were always the same. "Oh, Mother, my God, my God, my God, we are all going to prison. Make Daddy take him back, the poor boy. Mother, oh, my God, my God, Daddy take the boy back, leave him at the police station, take him to the FBI. They will understand. Oh, daddy, we are all going to prison."

Every time Willie Louise pleaded for her parents to do the right thing by me, Charlie would go into a rage and fisted Katie and Willie Louise, assuring them that they would be killed should they go to authorities. Many times, Charlie threatened to drown his wife and his daughter in their lake southwest of the barn if they ever said a word or went to the authorities.

REVEREND DON WESLEY HUSTED, SR.

1939 – At 17000 Nebraska Street, Kansas City, Kansas, the Residence of Reverend Don Wesley Husted, Sr., and His Wife, Viola Mae Hoggett Husted

The time was early evening when Don Wesley Husted, Sr., and his wife, Viola, took me to an orphanage. The women were expecting us. Husted, Sr. attempted to lose me in this orphanage, insisting that they accept me. I remained overnight, but Viola was terribly stressed, and the woman at the orphanage demanded I be picked up. The motivation for his action was a mystery. When learning of her son's attempt to place me in an orphanage, Myrtle Husted lashed out angrily at her son. (We shared this house with rats, mice, and cockroaches).

1935 to 1944 - At 2101 South Oliver Street, Wichita, Kansas, the Residence of Loran McFadden Husted, and Myrtle Husted

Loren McFadden Husted and his wife Myrtle Husted took me with them to visit their relatives, attend family reunions, family member funerals, and on their vacations. Loren and Myrtle were calm, patient people, and I fit well into their lives by virtue of my being a silent child, calm, patient, and entertained myself with wholesome constructive projects, both personal and for school.

Two men in dark suits, white shirts, and black ties in a shiny black sedan followed us from a distance on many of our travels. When possible, the driver pulled alongside, then moved on. The passenger would observe me as well, often making eye contact with me. They had no problem observing me in that I was leaning on the back door looking at them with my face pressed against the rear window. I recall on one occasion the passenger shook his fist at Loren.

Another time, Loren stopped at a roadside gas station to fuel up and talked with a deputy sheriff. The two men pulled to a stop on the outer apron of the wide, dirt drive of the gas station, a two-pump Philip 66 station. Myrtle bought me an Orange Crush pop and Chiclets gum out of a machine.

Loren complained to the sheriff of being followed; the sheriff's deputy walked to the two men and returned to tell him there was no problem and no need for concern. Loren was growing nervous, high pitched and irritable. He placed his .38 Smith and Wesson revolver on the center of the front seat or in the glove compartment easily within his reach.

1939 – At 2101 South Oliver Street, Wichita, Kansas, the residence of Loren and Myrtle Husted

It was apparent that the FBI surveillance activity had stepped up. At 2101 South Oliver Street, Wichita, Kansas, a character in dark suit, white shirt, black tie, and driving a shiny black car would often sit a short distance north of the driveway, sometimes into the night.

Dorothy Mae Husted soon had a male companion who would pick up on her at work. He would not visit the family. He parked with Dorothy in front; he also wore a revolver in his shoulder holster.

Loren continued to call the Sheriff, who told him there was no problem. Loren was growing more nervous and anxious until he strapped on his shoulder holster pistol but was met with strong pleas from his wife not to confront the man in the auto. Both Myrtle and Dorothy often pleaded with Loren to avoid him. Dorothy described the man she was dating as someone who dressed in a dark suit, white shirt, and black tie. The auto was shiny black.

One late evening, Loren Husted walked to the car and demanded Dorothy to get out and come into the house. I stood on a kitchen stool, observing this activity through the basement window. Soon Dorothy had a new date, a tall well-dressed man. He was well accepted by Loren and Myrtle, and there was no interest in marriage.

The tall, well-dressed character worked at Boeing Aircraft. This gentleman talked to me, discussed my drawings, sketches, and doodles. He took several of them because he said he liked them.

1939 to 1940 - Scene Part Three, 2101 South Oliver Street, Wichita, Kansas, the Residence of Loren McFadden Husted, and Wife Myrtle Husted

Loren McFadden Husted and his wife, Myrtle Husted, weighed heavy on my mind. Cryptomnesia memory bloomed, generating an abundance of images in which I found the need to sketch. I wrote my name, Charles A. Lindbergh Jr. over and over. I covered my books, book covers, cardboard, pad, backs, wood boards, and the wood top shop stool with sketches and doodles from my past and my name. I easily sketched portraits of my mother, Anne Lindbergh, my father, Colonel Lindbergh, with and without his leather helmet and goggles, sketches of my nanny, Betty Gow, my grandmother Morrow, an Italian lady with black hair which could have been Teresa Capone, mother of Alphonse Capone and a beautiful Irish looking lady, like my former wife Kay, who might have been the wife of Alphonse Capone. I would write along the edges and on the pages of the sketches.

I sketched the face of an Italian man with hair parted in the center smoking a cigar, a long cigar. One impressive sketch was probably Sam Miano smoking a pipe. I painted this sketch on the wood seat of a shop stool. I also did sketches of the Roosevelt Field Aircraft Hanger and several early airplanes.

These sketches held the attention of the tall man from Boeing Aircraft. He was calm, quiet, and said very little. This tall well-dressed character from Boeing was interested in my aviation sketches, one being a three-power stage airship to the moon and a fuselage and wing design that years later came to be the design of the Boeing B47. This tall-dressed man took the airship and B47 sketches to Boeing.

My strong urge to sketch phased out in 1940. Between 1939 and 1944, I built balsa wood models of the Messerschmidt airplane, my favorite, a four-foot wingspan glider, and a five-foot longbow kit. The box kit, the glider, flew into space and vanished over Boeing Aircraft. I can do a rendition of all these sketches.

Charles A. Lindbergh, Jr. 1939

I REMEMBER, AND ALWAYS WILL

1934 to 1941 – At South Hillside Country School. An Estimated Four Miles from 2101 South Oliver Street, Down Mt. Vernon Road and Left on South Hillside to the Brick Schoolhouse

Kindergarten through grade four was taught in the basement of the South Hillside Country School. Grade five through grade twelve was taught in one room at ground level. The principal and teacher was Audrey Houston, wife of the owner of Houston Lumber Company. One day Mrs. Houston told the class that FBI special agents would be visiting. Soon afterward, two well-dressed FBI special agents visited and stood near Mrs. Houston's desk, which was in the northeast corner of the room to the left. As the three visited, Mrs. Houston pointed to me. I can draw a composite of the three faces as with many others whom I have met. My memory serves me well that way.

1934 to 1944 - The Airfield Terminal, Wichita Kansas- Could it be Myrtle Husted was Cooperating with FBI Special Agents?

Loren McFadden Husted and Bob Downing traveled the Rock Island RR to Monet and Joplin, Missouri, with an overnight stay in Monet, Missouri. On these weekends, Myrtle Husted would pack her picnic basket with fried chicken, olives stuffed with pimientos, homemade apple pie, chocolate milk, buttered biscuits, dill pickles or fresh ground ham salad sandwiches. Then she would take me to the airport.

We always located a spot on the lawn terrace to the left of the air terminal steps and left of the aircraft control tower crowned with a wind gauge. The air terminal door faced the runway, and the steps exited to the sidewalk along the storm fence and gate to the boarding and aircraft taxi area.

The aircraft hangar was to our front left opposite the aircraft taxi area. To the right of our position on the lawn, the terrace could be seen, the tall boarding step ramps, the baggage buggies, a fire truck, and a Philip 66 gas truck. The lawn terrace faced onto the boarding area where most the planes taxied. I enjoyed those occasions and always searched the faces of passengers coming in and boarding Braniff Airways, TWA, and the Lindbergh lines.

KEVIN HUSTED, SR.

1935 to 1944 - The Lawn Terrace of the Airfield Terminal, Wichita, Kansas

The many visits to the lawn terrace generated cryptomnesia activity. Myrtle and I would sit looking toward the aircraft taxi and boarding area. To our front left was the airfield aircraft banger. To our immediate right at the end of the sidewalk past the air, and the terminal steps was a white wood frame snack shop, and a red Coca Cola machine positioned against the snack shop wall on the driveway.

On our many visits to the lawn terrace, one or two men in dark suits, white shirts, black tie, and shined shoes in a black, shiny car pulled into the one car drive space between the sandstone, color brick air terminal, and the snack shop. I can still see them as they exited the shiny black car and I can see the top area of the red Coke machine through the car windows. These men walked in our direction stopping sometimes to the right of us at the storm fence, and then they turned often to observe me sitting on the lawn terrace.

Sometimes, these strangers would visit with Myrtle and several times asked if she would allow them to take me to the aircraft control tower. I vividly remember when I first went. One of them carried me to the glassed aircraft control tower; God is my witness; I am telling the truth.

In the tower, a man in a white shirt, and a black tie, wanted to examine my right leg and foot. I removed my right shoe and my sock, and he lifted my foot turning it side to side. When he let go, I slipped my shoe and sock back on. I can still see the strings being tied by that man.

39

Numerous times I was carried up and down the walkway and held up to the fence to observe the landing of an aircraft. As I grew older, I walked to the parked aircraft, which was to the left of the taxi area, and they placed me in the cockpit. I imagined my father sitting there with me as I could remember his face.

Often, they took me aboard a Braniff Airways plane. Beyond a shadow of a doubt, I knew I was being observed. Myrtle Husted, who kept an observant eye on my life, never seemed disturbed at their observant activity, nor do I recall her telling her husband, Loren, of our airfield adventures. I am not certain as to why she would keep this a secret; I just knew that it was.

While on the terrace, I often reflected a silhouette of my father walking to a plane and an image of the Roosevelt Field aircraft hangar. My obsession to search the faces of people accounts for my comprehension of the surveillance activity that has never left me causes me to wonder if my father ever saw me too.

1939 to 1940 - Living room, 2101 South Oliver Street, Wichita, Kansas, the Residence of Loran McFadden Husted, and Wife Myrtle Husted

I was doing homework assignments sitting at the dining room table. Myrtle cautiously approached Loren in the front room at the wide entrance area and said, "Loren, don't you think we should return the boy to his parents?"

Loren Husted snarled, "Colonel Lindbergh doesn't deserve a son; he's a Communist."

No more was said. I think Myrtle knew not to press the issue further.

KEVIN HUSTED, SR.

1934 to 1944 - Ruby's Rexall Drugstore, Harry Street and South Oliver Street, Wichita, Kansas

Jack Stuckey, the store manager of Ruby's Rexall Drugstore, put me to work as a busboy and dishwasher. I swept the floor and stacked wooden soda pop cases. I began to suffer terrible headaches, not sure why.

City buses going to and from Boeing loaded with wartime aircraft workers made lunchtime at the soda fountain a nightmare for orders of shredded beef sandwiches, malts, milkshakes, side dishes, coffee, and coffee to go.

Several times two men dressed in black suits, white shirts, and black ties, parked their shiny black car in front of the soda fountain windows. They would sit at the soda fountain just inside the door entrance and would ask the soda fountain woman manager, Mrs. Boyd, for the boy to wait on them. I served the two men black coffee. These men engaged in calm conversation and just kept looking at me.

Being a calm, patient lad with innate knowledge and wisdom to diligently perform all my responsibilities, I was well-liked for my getting the assigned jobs done with no conversation or complaints, and I did more than asked. The two men observing me engaged in conversation with my boss, Jack Stuckey, outside the door entrance. Jack Stuckey asked that I wash down all the outside front windows, which was odd since I had washed all of them the day before. I complied and began washing the widows. Halfway through the large windows, Jack said, "Pal, I am taking you fishing today. You can finish the windows tomorrow."

Jack Stuckey drove me to his residence, began packing up two fishing poles and gear, his wife made us sandwiches, and poured us both a glass of milk. That's when Jack told her, "The FBI thinks he is the Lindbergh boy."

Betty Stuckey looked at me, smiled, and seated me in the kitchen breakfast nook so they could have a private conversation. By then, it was too late. I heard what Jack said, which confirmed my belief all along. I felt helpless and knew I couldn't do anything about it, always wondering why my life had to be this way. Why didn't my father want me? I remember.

1943 - At 2101 South Oliver Street, Wichita, Kansas, the Residence of Loren McFadden Husted, and Wife Myrtle Husted

Loren and Myrtle Husted were engaged in a quiet conversation. Something was wrong, terribly wrong -- Myrtle communicated by phone with Viola Mae Hoggett Husted from El Dorado, Kansas.

The next morning, very early, Myrtle drove us to visit Viola. I was not allowed inside the house. Myrtle gave Viola money and several bags of groceries. Hence, on occasions through the years, Viola would say, "You're my boy. I was there when you were born; you best keep your mouth shut before you get yourself killed."

Her very words disturbed me because we were never close.

Often Myrtle would quietly instruct me, "When you grow up, you go see J. Edgar Hoover, Chief of the FBI. Mr. Hoover will help you. If you have trouble, you go to Mr. Hoover."

By 1944, this directive was very much established in my heart; I held indelible respect for J. Edgar Hoover and the FBI.

Viola Mae Hoggett Husted was given to a poor spirit and brutally dominated by Reverend Don Wesley Husted, Sr. Sadly, Viola was never physically strong and continuously hushed up because he often threatened to lock her up in the Lampard Kansas Mental Asylum for the insane.

MORE OF THE SAME WITH HUSTED SR.

1941 – At 331 North 30th Street, Kansas City, Kansas, a Resident of Reverend Don Wesley Husted, Sr., and Wife Viola Mae Hoggett Husted

KEVIN HUSTED, SR.

I lived with Reverend Don Wesley Husted, Sr., and each day was transported to Kansas City, Kansas, by train to attend schooling. For a short time, I attended Francis Willard School but would soon return to Wichita, Kansas.

The Sunday night following Saturday, March 1, 1941, Reverend Don Wesley Husted, Sr., attempted suicide. In the time frame of Saturday, March 1, 1941, through July 28, 1943, Husted, Sr. solicited in the *Kansas City Star* for paid passengers to California. After several interviews, Husted, Sr. told his mistress, Helen Conwell Rogers, "We will work our travel to California out of Wichita, Kansas."

I believed that two of the passengers were FBI agents. With this change in plan, Husted, Sr. decided to take me to visit his friends from 1939, who now lived in Henna, Wyoming.

From 1939 to 1943, the *Kansas City Star* ran many scandalous stories on Reverend Don W. Husted, Sr.

The week of Saturday, March 1, 1941, Husted, Sr, in Kansas City, Missouri, paid cash for a new black 1941 Mercury sedan. It is unknown how he disposed of the black Plymouth sedan. Husted, Sr, and his assistant pastor, Vince Parker, had for many weeks vigorously hyped the congregation to give monies.

Husted, Sr. collected thousands of dollars. The congregation was not aware, his wife Viola was not aware, and his assistant pastor was not aware that Husted, Sr. would soon vanish to California with his mistress, Helen Conwell Rogers.

Husted, Sr. postponed his escape until Christmas 1943 and in the meantime, worked his solicitation of paid passengers to California out of Wichita, Kansas. I have my theory about his motivation to visit Hanna, Wyoming. In his 1941 Mercury sedan, Husted, Sr., took me on his travels to Hanna, Wyoming.

To view over the dash, I sat on my small suitcase. As we traveled out of Kansas, I sensed we were being followed, and I quietly climbed in the back seat to look through the rear oval window. There it was, a shiny black car traveling a short distance back. I've seen that many times in my life, so I wasn't overly concerned. Given to an innate code of silence but a state of being aware and observant, miles passed, many miles, when I suddenly sensed Husted, Sr. casting glances in the door's side mirror, and then to the center rearview mirror. Husted, Sr. demanded that I lay down on the back seat. He had a problem with my doing so because I would peek over the backseat to see if we were still being followed.

Husted, Sr., who never spent a dime on me for clothes, shoes, ice cream, etc., told me he would buy me a pair of cowboy boots. I was excited because from July 22, 1941, to July 26, 1941, was the Cheyenne Rodeo. I would attend it in a pair of new cowboy boots.

So, Husted, Sr. took me with him into the downtown area bumper to bumper Cheyenne Rodeo traffic; the black car followed. As luck would have it, Husted, Sr. moved into a space in front of a western store; my eyes were fixed on the black car, and I watched the driver pull the black sedan into a space about three or four cars back. The man exited his car, put on his coat, and with his eyes fixed on me, held me determined in his sight. The man inched his way through the crowded sidewalk. The tall

FBI agent and I made eye contact; I could tell he wasn't about to lose me in the crowd.

I was looking back at the tall man as Husted, Sr. dragged me from the car into the western store and seated me. I faced the entrance to the crowded western store with my eyes fixed on the door waiting for the tall man, and there he was. He walked through the door stopping short of me by several feet to the rear of Husted, Sr. He gazed at me, his eyes fixed on me, and I observed him as my boots were being fitted by the sales clerk. Husted, Sr., paid for the boots as the man moved through the door.

When I had my new boots, we left the western store. Just as I stepped onto the sidewalk, the man who observed me entered the black car.

Husted, Sr. did not look at the man. He demanded I lie down on the car floorboard, which was an impossibility for me because of my size.

As Husted, Sr. moved into traffic, so did the man in the black car. Husted Sr. was tense and suddenly took a quick turn into an alleyway on his right, and the chase began through side streets.

The chase continued for a long while until the man in the black car got caught in dense traffic. Husted, Sr. pulled up alongside a park, engine running, until he felt that we had lost the man in the black car.

After that, Husted Sr. moved us to Hanna, Wyoming. At the Hanna, Wyoming residence of George and Erby Trent, Husted, Sr. never discussed being followed. Most likely we were followed to Hanna, Wyoming.

1943 – At 331 North 30th Street, Kansas City, Kansas, the Residence of Reverend Don Wesley Husted, Sr., and Wife Viola Mae Hoggett Husted

I was placed on the train for Wichita, Kansas, and soon re-enrolled in Hillside Country School. Husted, Sr. told his mistress, Helen Conwell Rogers, he was receiving calls from the two men wishing to travel to California he believed to be FBI agents. Husted, Sr. canceled the phone line.

Next, I saw Husted, Sr. just before Christmas in 1943. He was soliciting paid passengers to California.

1943 – At 2101 South Oliver Street, Wichita, Kansas, The Residence of Loren McFadden Husted, and Wife Myrtle Husted

It was around Christmas time. Loren Husted was furious at his son, Husted, Jr. Husted, Sr told Myrtle, "Raise him yourself; he's not my kid. I'm not going to raise the boy."

Loren demanded I go with him to California; Myrtle demanded I remain with her. He then told his son, "Don't do anything for the boy."

The time was early morning, and I hid between a wood post and the Lennox furnace A/C listening to Loren Husted and his son engaged in conversation about my not being his son and that he had no intention of raising me, and then there was a conversation over a large sum of money. I'm not sure where the money came from, I only knew that Husted, Sr. had it.

1943 – Myrtle Husted Took Me on a Visit to the Sigmans in El Dorado, Kansas

The Katie Sigman relations were holding a family reunion. Carrie Mitchell Smith was a well-recognized psychic known for her intuitions and for being accurate. Carrie told Katie, "He is the Lindbergh boy."

Myrtle and I cut our visit short, returning to Wichita, Kansas. On numerous occasions, Carrie had told Katie Sigman that I was the Lindbergh boy. Each time I overheard their conversations, my heart broke as I longed to hear from my father to ask him one question, "Why don't you come and get me? What did I do so wrong?"

1944 - Commodore Apartments, 685 South Lucas, Los Angeles, California 90617

Reverend Don Wesley Husted, Sr. and his mistress, Helen Conwell Rogers took me to their eleventh story apartment in Los Angeles. I was given the address and phone number and told to catch the Glendale Trolley at Wilshire Blvd and 7th Street and to ask the trolley captain to tell me when we got to Glendale High School. I could say I was without fear having been kidnapped and having lived a life packed with pluses and minuses. By this time, I had figured out most of everything except why my father never came for me.

At Glendale High School, a school of 5,000 students, I experienced real fear. I spent the first day locating a classroom and quickly exited as two zoot suits pulled switchblades on each other, and the teacher went to get help. On my way out, I saw that the office was a jam of students. I snuck out of school and lost myself on the school grounds uncertain how to return home by trolley.

A Chinese boy saw that I was lost and invited me to his home located behind a Chinese restaurant owned by his parents. This was my first taste of Chinese food, and I liked it.

Soon, I was on the phone to Husted, Sr. and we agreed that it was best if I stayed overnight with this family.

Finally, I made my way home by mid-afternoon the next day and never returned to Glendale High School.

The next day came. It was early morning, Husted, Sr., and his mistress, Helen, were having breakfast. He and Helen both assured me that they had no intention of raising me, and I best tow the line, follow their rules or be shipped off to reform school.

Husted, Sr, told me, "At midnight we leave for San Luis Obispo, California. You are to call Helen, Mother and never mention Kansas, never mention Don Jr., Richard, or Judy."

Sinister parents and sinister people themselves, they thought their children were equally corrupt or crooked. I accepted his harsh instructions well short of planning to follow his orders.

COLONEL CHARLES A. LINDBERGH, SR.

❦

1944 – At 1118 Buchon Street, San Luis Obispo, California. Residence of Reverend Don Wesley Husted, Sr., and His Mistress Now Known to be Helen Husted

Repeatedly assured by Husted, Sr., that I was not welcomed, and he would never accept me contributed to my growing more self-reliant and self-contained.

Johnny, the telegram Tribune Newspaper dispatcher for paper routes, hired me to deliver a 250-customer route, no matter the heat, wind, rain, or cold. I managed this paper route well, with deliveries and collections at $44 per month average income. My customers made my 1944 Christmas the best since the Christmas of 1939. To earn extra money, I cut lawns and washed store windows along Monterey Street and Higuera Street and soon had built a credible reputation with merchants as doing a job well and being of good character.

Washing merchant store windows netted odd jobs for a few dollars in addition to an hourly daily job sacking potatoes for O.G. Pennington Grocery Store, I scrubbed down sidewalks at other storefronts. When washing down the windows of Austin's, I would wipe dry the wood and marble trim, and polish the brass doorknobs. Owner Charles Simon and his wife owned Austin's Candy Kitchen, which was a soda fountain and restaurant famous for quality candies, foods, and service.

The Simons asked me to work for them. I accepted and worked three years after school and on Saturdays and Sundays. The Simons approved me to be the cleanest and most diligent bus and fountain boy who they ever had hired. At first, I could barely reach the soda fountain countertop and grew into the job.

One early bright, sunny morning, Charles Simon bolted through the front door in a brisk walk pointing to me as he passed the counter on his way to his office, and said, "Come with me, take off your hat and jacket."

Mr. Simon summoned Mrs. Simon from the kitchen; she entered the office as I was hanging up my white jacket and hat. With the office door ajar, I listened to Charles Simon tell Mrs. Simon that the FBI thinks that I was the Lindbergh boy. He said, "I'm taking the boy to Red Corcoran's Coffee Shop to meet the FBI, Jim Hannah, and Colonel Lindbergh."

I felt my stomach drop thinking that my father had come for me.

Just then, Mrs. Simon stepped from the office, took my hands in hers, and gazed into my face with awe. It was like she was studying me. Then Charles Simon came out and said, "You're going with me to Red Corcoran's Coffee Shop, some people want to see you. You can have anything you like."

"I would like a pineapple milkshake," I responded.

We made our way to Red Corcoran's Coffee Shop.

The FBI special agent greeted Mrs. Simon and pulled me back to the front counter stool as I started to walk to an empty table. It was then that I saw my father, the Colonel. I knew it was him. I remembered his face that was etched in my mind.

The FBI special agent seated me on the first stool and asked Mr. Simon to take a seat to my left. The FBI agent stood in front of me.

Red Corcoran himself operated the soda fountain and worked behind the counter that had a back smokey-glass mirror. I ordered a pineapple milkshake from him just as I earlier said I wanted. To view the FBI special agent, Jim Hannah, and my father, Colonel Lindbergh, I had to do some leaning stretching forward and backward to catch a glimpse in the mirror. I really only wanted to look at my father, but Red Corcoran moved to block my view.

Charles Simon was more than six feet tall and weighed approximately two hundred and seventy-five pounds. I had to stretch to peek at my father.

The FBI agent smiled and asked me, "What would you like to be when you grow up?"

"An FBI agent or a doctor," I replied as I stretched again to peek at my father.

I remember, with one eye the Colonel would glance at me from the back of Jim Hannah's head.

Charles Simon dismissed us, and kindly herded me through the door and around the corner to Austin's not allowing me to view or talk with my father.

I returned to work upset; I wanted to leave and go back to Red Corcoran's. I wanted to confront the man whom I believed and knew in my heart was my father. My desire was overwhelming.

A short measure of time passed when Charles Simon told me Red Corcoran called asking if I could wash his store windows.

I replied, "He has his own boy who washes his windows. What does he need me for?"

"He likes your work."

"Are you okay with me doing his windows?"

That was easy; I don't think he had a choice in the matter because I was told I would be washing Red Corcoran's window.

When I arrived At Red Corcoran's storefront, Mr. Corcoran was in front of the windows with a bucket of soapsuds, a scrubber, and squeegee. He didn't say much as he handed me the window washing bucket. I started immediately.

Shortly after that, a man dressed in Khaki came out the door and walked north as I continued to scrub. When working the squeegee slowly, calmly, and thoroughly down and across the window, I suddenly sensed being watched. I stopped, looked to my right, which was north. And, there he was a storefront away, my father, Colonel Lindbergh, observing me. I remember from deep within me bloomed a glow, a warm kinship glow like a baby gets when greeted by a kind parent. I wanted to run toward my father, but I couldn't move. We just kept looking at each other. I will never forget his face or his eyes as they gazed upon me. I think he knew I was his son, but for whatever reason couldn't or wouldn't tell me. It broke my heart, and I felt isolated and helpless.

He began to walk away, stopped, turned to observe me, walked toward me, then stopped. Without even a smile or a nod, he then walked north away from me, and every couple of steps, he glanced back over his shoulder and looked at me as he walked. I could not take my eyes off my father. I remember that I didn't finish the windows and left the bucket and tools on the sidewalk. I wanted to follow my father, but it was too late; he had disappeared from my sight. So, I returned to Austin's with a broken heart.

ALL IN A DAYS WORK

1944 - Austin's Soda Fountain Counter, San Luis Obispo, California – Months Later

I was working the soda fountain counter at Austin's when Jim Hanan walked in with father, Colonel Lindbergh. The two sat in front of the soda carbonate spigots. Jim asked for two cups of coffee. After serving the coffee, I leaned back on the wooden counter, my heart pounded, and it was if I became frozen and unable to speak.

My father would not look up into my face. He raised his eyebrows and glanced and then looked toward the rear of the store. Jim Hanan would look up to observe my face, then turn to his to the right in a quiet conversation with my father. I never could get up my nerve to confront him. The two stayed for a good measure of time, and then walked out without speaking to me.

In the days following that visit, Jim Hanan would visit me. One time he asked me if I would like to be a Sea Scout and invited me to his residence.

KEVIN HUSTED, SR.

1944 to 1947 - Austin's Restaurant, San Luis Obispo, California

In hushed tones, I heard the murmurings from others that I was possibly the Lindbergh boy. The possibility of me being the Lindbergh boy traveled fast among the merchants. Nightly en route to perform surgeries, Doctor Edison French, M.D. Surgeon, founder of French Clinic, stopped to be served a hot chocolate topped with marshmallows. Always leaving a silver dollar under the saucer, Dr. French observed me as well.

Charles A. Lindbergh, Jr.

The Austins nightly dined at the soda fountain counter. Mrs. Simon, her parents, the Burgess family, also dined with the Simons and engaged in conversation. I overheard Mr. Burgess say, "He looks like a Lindbergh." Mr. Burgess was certain that I was.

Downtown merchants were furious when they learned Husted, Sr., took all my earnings from my paper route.

Charles Simon caught Husted, Sr. in a Hart Shaftner Mark suit a storefront away waiting to take my earnings. Charles Simon assured Husted, Sr. he would blacklist him among the merchants. Mr. Simon did so.

One summer, I worked stocking hay in Templeton, California. When the season ended, after this arduous experience under the hot sun, I was relieved to go to work as a stock boy for Montgomery Ward across from

Austin's. The Simons were deeply hurt but agreed a change would be good, and I was welcomed to return any time I chose.

The employees at Montgomery Ward were longtime on the job, and many of them conversed on my being the son of Lindbergh. My boss was Pres Helms, a diligent supervisor with two adult sons.

On early Saturday mornings, the Cotanneo cousins would pick up the trash in a German green truck with high sides. One of them, Charles Cotanneo, died in 1998. These two individuals would sing Sicilian ballads as they worked on Monterey Street and Higuera Street.

One Saturday as I was unloading stock from a Model T pickup, my boss, Mr. Helms, was standing to my right when the Cotanneo cousins, breaking down boxes from atop the truck, yelled, "Lindbergh, when you grow up, we're going to put you in the Mafia."

Shaking his hands to hush them, Mr. Helms said, "Hush, he doesn't know."

He may think that I didn't know, but by then, I had an inkling of my true identity.

The Cotanneo brothers laughed Mr. Helms off, and one of them said to me, "Lindbergh, we like you, you're a good kid, and one day you can work for us."

During the 1969-1970 investigations, I met the Cotanneo cousins, their pal Joe Minafo, in the Hyatt House lobby, San Jose, California.

KEVIN HUSTED, SR.

1944 to 1951 - Arroyo Grande, California, Fair Oaks District, the Residence of Reverend Don Wasley Husted, Sr., and Wife Helen Husted

The 1947-1948 FBI surveillance activity persisted. Henry Faulstich, the owner of Faulstich Brothers Brick Works, hired me to work through the summer of 1947 and the summer of 1948 at $2.75 per hour with double pay for overtime, altogether about $725.00 a month. I operated the dirt vibrator sifter high over the auger box, an estimated twenty steps high. I was well insulated.

My boss, Joe Silva, was a foreman of longstanding. He demanded top performance, and my job was guaranteed by virtue of the quality of dirt sifted. The sifter screen demanded continuous attention until Joe blew the whistle at noon and at the end of the day.

Lunch could be under a eucalyptus tree, atop of pallet of bricks, or in the shade of the tool shed office. Joe Silva would call me Lindbergh, and over a brown bag, lunch would talk about my father's flights. One day an FBI agent pulled into the brickyard and spoke with Joe. I was atop the sifter but had a great vantage point. Periodically during their conversation, Joe pointed to me. The FBI agent stood around for a while frequently looking up to me.

The Cousins

A short distance northeast of the Husted, Sr. residence, lived the two cousins and their families. I paid $1.00 daily to ride roundtrip with these two who worked at Faulstich Brothers on the auger and fresh brick belt.

These cousins clearly communicated they were related to an FBI agent, someone who was probably their cousin by the name of Sample. These two were smart hillbillies; the two called me Lindbergh or Charles.

I never discussed with the two cousins the terrible brutalities I endured at the hands of Husted, Sr. nor his demand of my paychecks, but the two cousins assured me they would punch out him should he beat me up again. They didn't like my situation at all. These two boasted that they had information on me, and I gave consideration these two may have been working uncover.

Joe Silva assured me, "If Don Husted, Sr. drove into the brickyard, I would lay him out flat. Lindbergh, you let me know if he ever lays a hand on you. I'll kill the bastard."

At least someone had my back.

1950 to 1951 - North Hatchery, North Broiler Farm and Purina Feed Co, San Luis Obispo, CA

By the credible reputation of my merchant friends, I was put to work by Mr. North, who assigned me a time-managed schedule. Mr. North and I had communicated on my desire to enroll at Stanford University so that I could become a doctor. In high school, I earned A, A+, and B+ on studies of the eye, ear, brain, and heart.

Both Mr. North and Dr. Edison French, M.D. were aware that Reverend Don W. Husted, Sr., and his wife were both vigorously opposed to my enrolling at Stanford University and did not approve of my having secretly joined the USN Reserve. This action caused

Husted, Sr. with his friends to enter the San Luis Obispo Selective Service Board in a rage, shouting threats to the recruiters.

The Hatchery

My accepting the North Hatchery job meant moving from the residence of Reverend Don W. Husted, Sr. and his wife, Helen. Mr. North provided me a bedroom in the hatchery. A large emergency bell mounted over the inside door connected to the Honeywell Hatch cabinet power source. Mr. North educated me in my responsibility of hatch temperature controls, culling the hatched chicks, clearing up the waste, and the Purina feed nutritional value for broilers, wild game, and calves.

On hatch days, I culled chicks. I also transported these peeping chicks to the broiler farm in Santa Maria, California. One day a week, I loaded 500 bags of Purina broiler feed, unloaded at the broiler farm hatches of between 30,000-50,000 birds and steam blasted clean the Honeywell hatch cabinets. Certain culled chicks I was allowed to keep in the back pen, and these I fed pheasant feed.

The hatchery bedroom evidenced my 1932-1934 impressions of inherited Italian characteristics. The nondescript room had a single bed frame and mattress, a basin, a mirror, and a clothes hanger post. A small dresser, a square-top wood table, and a funnel-shaped porcelain green, white shade hung down over the table.

I REMEMBER

Italian Memories

My earliest Italian memories from 1932 to 1934 were revealed by my choosing to cover the table with a red and white check tablecloth, some salami, a block of cheese, a buck knife, a bar glass, and a bottle of red wine. My rifle was leaned against the wall to the right of the hard bed.

Commander Steve Gatti

On two flights, I flew with Commander Steve Gatti, USN Reserve (Boeing B47 test pilot). On both trips, I enjoyed flying in the co-pilot seat of a USN twin Beech taildragger. Commander Gatti would fly the twin Beech through its maximum ability in dives. On my last flight with Commander Gatti, as we approached the Wichita Air Field and were about to touchdown, the tower observer blurted a clear warning message that the landing gears were in the up position. In split seconds Commander Gatti scooped air up and on a right leg returned for landing with the landing gears down and locked.

Around this same time, the Ninth Naval District Commander assigned me to letter, paint, and gold leaf an eight-foot sign of Navy gold wings Ninth Naval District. The sign was mounted at the entrance of the Glenview, Illinois Naval Base.

1951 - Guy Stearman, the Functional Test Lab, Boeing Aircraft Co, Wichita, Kansas. (12:00 Midnight through 8:00 a.m. shift)

On occasion, I rested in the parachute loft, and when not running PSI tests or editing specifications, I would do homework in the office of Guy Stearman.

Often, retired USMC Colonel Guy Stearman, and I visited over our brown bag homemade lunches. Myrtle Husted always prepared a tasty lunch that reminded me of the picnic lunches we had enjoyed long ago on the lawn terrace of the Wichita airfield terminal. Over lunches, Guy Stearman would tell of his short-lived combat flying.

During one of the USMC fighter flights, he was shot down by a Japanese pilot and placed in a Japanese prisoner of war camp for the remainder of the war to which he attributed his habit of fast devouring sandwiches.

Colonel Guy Stearman avoided discussing my father, Colonel Lindbergh, Sr.

In the lab, Richard Gardener and Melvin McGuire, both test engineers, would ponder at my being the Lindbergh boy.

I was often observed, and many times asked to stop doing the functional test to visit with Melvin McGuire, Richard Gardener, and a person named Bill Ward. They were visited by a man named Grady, who either dressed in Khaki or dark blue trousers, a windbreaker jacket, or sometimes a blue or black suit. He always wore black socks and shoes. Bill Ward, Melvin McGuire, and Grady would often try to get me dreaming about owning a big sailboat.

McGuire would yell, "Hey, Lindbergh!"

The three would then laugh.

Jane Buckman

Jane Buckman was an Assistant RN to Mrs. Dougherty, RN in charge of the Boeing Medical First Aid Station. When word was out, I would marry Jane Buckman, RN, Bill Ward, and Melvin McGuire attempted to discourage my marrying. They would say things such as, "Grady and the FBI don't like her, that gal is a bitch."

Husted, Sr. arrived in a matter of a few minutes and immediately began brutally to sling his fist and kick me. This fight was the closest I have ever come to killing someone. As I cooled, I packed my rifle in the wood footlocker, nailed on the lid, and with one Indian head nickel in my pocket, I walked down the highway to the Arroyo Grande, California Greyhound bus terminal.

KEVIN HUSTED, SR.

1951 - Greyhound Bus Terminal, Arroyo Grande, California

Mr. Lund, the Greyhound bus dispatcher, summoned the deputy sheriff from the bar next door. The deputy sheriff was as furious as was Mr. Lund on seeing me; my face, hands, arms, and body were bruised, swollen and bloody. The deputy sheriff was known for using his sap and visited Husted, Sr. several times at the request of neighbors who complained of my being abused.

1951 – At 2101 South Oliver Street, Wichita, Kansas, the Residence of Loren, and Myrtle Husted

Mr. Lund visited by phone with Myrtle Husted, who agreed to pay my bus fare from Wichita, Kansas. At Phoenix, I bought a Babe Ruth candy bar with the Indian head nickel. Three nights later, I arrived in Wichita, Kansas on a Trailways bus.

Myrtle Husted was waiting there for me. En route to their home, we stopped for hamburgers at Baum's Hamburger Stand, then Cero's Candy Kitchen for a chocolate malt. At their residence, Myrtle and Loren shared their shock as I stripped to my shorts. From head to toe, my torso was a massive medieval artwork of bruises, bumps, and dried blood.

I showered, we had prayer, and I went to bed for a good night's sleep, but not before I listened to Myrtle and Loren, who called their son and vigorously reprimanded him for his misdeeds. My physical condition was more critical than from any of the many previous beatings.

The morning began with their prayer time and a hearty breakfast. Myrtle Husted traveled me to several downtown stores for new clothes and shoes. She gave me some cash and key to the house.

Days passed before my face was back to normal. In the garage workshop was the wood top shop stool, painted with the face of Sam Miano smoking a pipe. It took me to my memory of many sketches of my mother, Anne Lindbergh, my father Colonel Lindbergh, the Roosevelt field aircraft hangar, and the faces of characters previously mentioned. I visited by phone with Charlie Sigman and Katie.

Myrtle Husted traveled me to visit with Charlie Sigman and wife Katie; Willie Louise was away.

Charlie and I traveled to visit the Ford dealership, where he bought me a new–like used two-door 1941 Mercury Club Coupe. He would not talk to me about the early days, nor would he allow me to go into the posh parlor room or the bunkhouse bedroom. He did tell me, however, that I would share in his estate. "You are like my son," he said.

Yet his generosity quickly vanished after Willie Louise gave birth to a daughter, Georgia Young, in 1952, and our communications ended.

I enrolled at El Dorado Junior College, now Butler County Community College. I applied for a transfer to the Ninth Naval District USN Reserve Squadron 228 from the Twelfth Naval District at Treasure Island, CA.

Both Charlie Sigman and Katie evidenced anxiety on my visits. I did look at the brown on brown Hudson stored in the single garage and the saddle tack house.

For some time, I viewed the interior of the brown on brown Hudson sport coupe. Cryptomnesia memory blooms traveled me back to flashes of our travel from Chicago, Illinois, a stop at a one-pump Crown Gas Station, and the 1935 predawn travel to 241 South Volutsia Street, Wichita, Kansas.

Katie and Willie Louise had gone over a culvert damaging the coupe. I shut the garage door, then visited the closed down roadhouse crossing the peanut field where once people met to gamble on Sunday at the Greyhound dog races.

More Threats

The Selective Service Board headquarters mailed more threats. In the time frame of Charles Sigman buying the 1941 Mercury Club Coupe, Charlie and I discussed the threats from the Selective Service Board and my one hundred percent attendance in the USN Reserve.

The Selective Service Board threatened me with prosecution on the grounds that I had joined the USN Naval Reserve to avoid the draft, which I did with vigorous support from Chief Warrant Officer Stahl and Lt. Cmdr. Vance Lewis. Charles Sigman called his pal Harry Truman, and I explained to Mr. Truman I had one hundred percent attendance in the USN Reserve.

Mr. Truman agreed that was acceptable but added, "Are you afraid of getting killed?"

He was a wise guy.

Charlie Sigman continued visiting with his pal Harry Truman after he had asked me to step outside.

THE CALL OF DUTY

1951 - Rural Route One, Butler County, Kansas, El Dorado, Kansas

In mid-October 1952, I visited Charlie and Katie Sigman at the bunkhouse kitchen, where I held in my arms their only grandchild, Georgia Louise Young.

On visiting the main house where Willie Louise, now a beautician, was at work with a lady under the dryer, Willie Louise again evidenced a measure of hysteria. In a hushed tone, she began saying to her mother, "Oh, my God, we are all going to prison. What are we going to do?"

Katie Sigman told her, "Hush or your father will kill us."

At this time, Charlie was in the bunkhouse kitchen caring for his granddaughter, Georgina Louise Young.

USN Reserve

In the time frame of buying the 1941 Mercury sport coupe and enrollment in Butler Country Naval District

USN Reserve Commander, M. L. Detter, worked at Boeing Aircraft co., and U.S. Naval Reserve Squadron 228, Executive Officer, Lt. Commander Danny Carl, worked in the Functional Test Department. I soon learned I was the only Seaman recruit to fly with Squadron 228.

Squadron 228 - Top Guns!

Squadron 228 consisted of Commander M. L. Detter, USN Reserve; Lt. Commander Danny Carl, USN Reserve; Lt. Commander Mac Snavely, USN Reserve; Lt. Commander Steve Gatti, USN Reserve (a Boeing 547 test pilot); Lt. Commander Avery, USN Reserve; Lt. Commander Harry Beu, USN Reserve; Loren Paul Husted (Charles A. Lindbergh, Jr.); and USN Reserve. Lt. Commander Danny Carl.

Commander Danny Carl set me up to apply to the Naval Academy with influence from Lt. Commander Harry Beu.

USN Reserve Lt. Commander Harry Beu was a key member of the Ninth Naval District headquarters in Olathe, Kansas. Lt. Commander Danny Carl often took me in a Navy SNJ to fly over Kansas, Iowa, and Missouri. Danny taught me to fly. During many Sundays, we flew formation at 10,000 feet.

I frequently flew with Lt. Commander Harry Beu. On one occasion, we flew to film the floodwaters that destroyed the Fairfax District of Kansas City, Missouri. We filmed gushing waters, twisting steel bridges, and many destroyed houses. As we flew over the gushing floodwaters of the Kau River, I sat on the right side in view of Lt. Commander Harry Beu and to the rear of a distinguished USN Commander in the copilot seat.

The Commander and Lt. Commander Beu openly discussed my being the Lindbergh boy. Lt. Commander Beu said, "He doesn't know," as he glanced at me to his rear right.

The twin Beech engines were loud but did not drown out the verbal resonance.

At Olathe, Kansas Naval Base, in this time frame, I met both John Kennedy and Commander George Bush, a pal of Lt. Commander Harry Beu. I was treated no less than as an officer. I worked the flight checklist before takeoff and made sure all fuel tanks were topped out.

The Selective Service Board continued to send threatening letters. I burned the letters on the advice of Lt. Commander Harry Beu, USN Reserve, and Lt. Commander Danny Carl who assured me the Selective Broad had no power to enforce their threats.

1951 - Guy Stearman, the Functional Test Lab, Boeing Aircraft Co., Wichita, Kansas (Midnight Through Early Morning)

One morning early between 2:00 a.m. and 3:00 a.m. toward the end of my successful work experience in Functional Test, Guy Stearman, Danny Carl, Richard Gardner, Melvin McGuire, and I were listening to Boeing B47 test pilot Lt. Commander Steve Gatti and two Air Force pilots on a routine B47 test run. Lt. Commander Gatti was flying an Air Force owned Boeing-owned B47. The forward landing gear of the U.S. Air Force B47 would not drive into place.

Lt. Commander Steve Gatti pulled his B47 up under the other B47 to investigate the well- lighted landing gear well. In split seconds of passing over the Boeing plant, there was a terrific explosion. The air streamed sucked the two B47 planes together causing a crash northeast of Beech Aircraft.

Lt. Commander Danny Cart and I drove over to the site arriving shortly before dawn. Debris was blown for many miles. There were many firemen, fire trucks, police, and deputy sheriffs. All the pilots were burned to death.

The torso of Steve Gatti was in the blackened fuselage. A little after this tragic accident, I moved with Jane Buckman, now my wife to Iowa.

JOHN DEERE

1952 to 1956 - John Deere Planter Works, Moline, Illinois

Prior to joining the John Deere Planter Works, I was employed at the Pioneer Seed Corn Company. My boss was retired USN Lt. Commander Knottingham. I worked the corn sheller belt where, on more than one occasion, two FBI special agents observed me. At lunch one day, the boss told me President Harry S. Truman would soon pass by on the train. All of us met the train that passed about one hundred feet from the corn sheller belt. In this same time frame, FBI special agent Peterson, whose father lived in West Liberty, Iowa, had been in communications with my father-in-law, Ray Buckman.

It was 8:00 a.m., Tuesday, November 18, 1952, when I received a call from the personnel director, Lloyd Rasmussen, at the John Deere Planter Works telling me I had passed the Deere & Co. physical examination and welcoming me to report to Mr. John E. Hoffman, Vice President, the plant manager.

I promptly visited John Hoffman in his executive suite. A calm, patient, well-dressed man who was also a graduate of Iowa State University.

Later, Mr. Ames, a top executive, welcomed me on board. Mr. Hoffman briefed me on my responsibilities and what was to be expected of me. He also informed me about their corporate no deductible major medical insurance and retirement benefits. My wages were $228 monthly x 1.26% cost of living increase for a total at $287.28. My pay increases and bonuses for valued innovations would be determined in quarterly performance evaluations.

During the medical examination, the physician suggested I join the Doric Masonic Lodge, "You being a Mason is to your advantage; Deere & Co is Masonic."

The aromas of Swedish food cooking rose from the second-floor kitchen as Mr. Hoffman and I began my tour of the plant department. A short measure of time before lunch we arrived in the prototype product design department. Mr. Hoffman introduced me to William P. "Bill" Oehler, Chief Product Engineer. Mr. Hoffman excused himself and said he would meet us for lunch.

William P. "Bill" Ochler provided me a tour of the product design department where I met A. J. Immesote, engineer, Charlie Youngberg, Harold Hansen, engineer, Clarence Danner, draftsman, Perry Ford, Ed Minor, and others. I was then assigned a large draftsman table by Mr. Oehler and received his warm welcome.

The stairwell and file cabinets, and a green merchant calculator divided product design from tool and die engineering. The quality control department was to the far- left rear and closed in. The blacksmith shop was outside the product design department.

At noon we joined all the staff in the dining room to enjoy the exceptional Swedish dishes. The Swedish potato sausage was my first. I sat by retired Lt. Colonel Guy W. Ade who also welcomed me to product design.

In 1947 Lt. Colonel Guy W. Ade, G2 Provost Marshall Pacific Theater had flown with General Billy Mitchell, a friend of Illinois Governor Adlai Stevenson, Illinois Congressman Douglas Black, and also a friend of General Jimmy Doolittle.

In 1955 Lt. Colonel Ade was voted President of the U.S. Philanthropic Society. At John Deere Planter Works, Moline, Illinois, he was a cost analyst for prototype product design. He was also a Mason in the Doric Masonic Lodge. Lt. Colonel Ade was calm, patient, authoritarian, and chose well the words he used to express his thoughts. He was unpretentious and cherished his wife and son, Ralph Ade, who was attending the University of Chicago Medical University. He had lost his oldest son in a freak accident on the Normandy Beachhead. A no-nonsense character, Colonel Ade and wife accepted my son, Craig, and I like we were family. I kindly declined the Colonel's kind offer to sponsor me in the Doric Masonic Lodge.

Lt. Colonel Ade gave me a book entitled *1001 Mechanical Designs*, a series of math books by International Institute and several valued drawing tools. Chief Engineer Bill Oehler gave me a list of required drawing tools.

The four years of high school mechanical drawing and architecture instruction, where I received continuous recognition for creating a precision drawing, was about to be applied. At my draftsman table, I kept hard lead pencils needlepoint sharp and worked my measurement on mechanical designs at 1/64 of an inch.

From November 18, 1952, through May 6, 1956, forty-one months, Lt. Colonel Guy W. Ade, and I invested the hour lunchtime break brainstorming for solutions to unsolved developments in prototype products These brainstorming activities earned me wage increases and bonuses each in excess of five hundred dollars.

1953 - John Deere Planter Works, Moline, Illinois.

The San Luis Obispo, California Selective Service Board had stepped up their vigorous threats to prosecute me and finally demanded I report to San Francisco, California. The 9th Naval District Commandant through the Des Moines, Iowa Commander, the Governor of Iowa, was my squadron leader. Lt. Commander Otis Jenks (an executive with American Can Co.), advised me to ignore the threats, "Burn the letter," he said.

I took his advice and burned the letter. Lt. Colonel Ade asked me to give him the next letter, saying, "I'll stop the bastards. I'll pull rank!"

Through Illinois Congressman Douglas Black, Lt. Colonel Ade transferred my Selective Service file from San Luis Obispo, California, to Chicago, Illinois. Then the Lt. Colonel told me the file was lost forever. That was the end of the vigorous effort to prosecute me. I continued my U.S. Naval Reserve duty at 100%

attendance and was honorably discharged after six years, ten months, and five days from 1948 to 1955.

1953 - John Deere Planter Works, Moline, Illinois

John Deere Planter Works Chief Engineer William P. 'Bill' Oehler, Personnel Director Lloyd Rasmussen, and Vice President/Plant General Manager, John E. Hoffman received continual anonymous phone calls throughout my years at John Deere Planter Works.

Mr. Oehler, Mr. Rasmussen, Mr. Hoffman, and Colonel Ade all assured me that my job position was not threatened. In late 1954, Lt. Colonel Ade disclosed to me the nature of the anonymous calls. The Lt. Colonel first told me the matter was being investigated. He then asked, "Does Husted, Sr., have a life insurance policy on you?"

"Yes," I replied. "Fifteen thousand whole life with the Canada Life Assurance Company."

I brought the policy to the Lt. Colonel, and the Affidavit of Beneficiary change was prepared from Beneficiary Don Wesley Husted, Sr., to my son, Paul Craig Husted.

Lt. Colonel Ade said, "Husted, Sr., plans to get rid of you. I know why the two FBI agents visited me. They were the ones you saw sitting with me this morning. They will be returning. Some time ago, I sent a letter to General Spear at the Pentagon. I'll soon have some information for you."

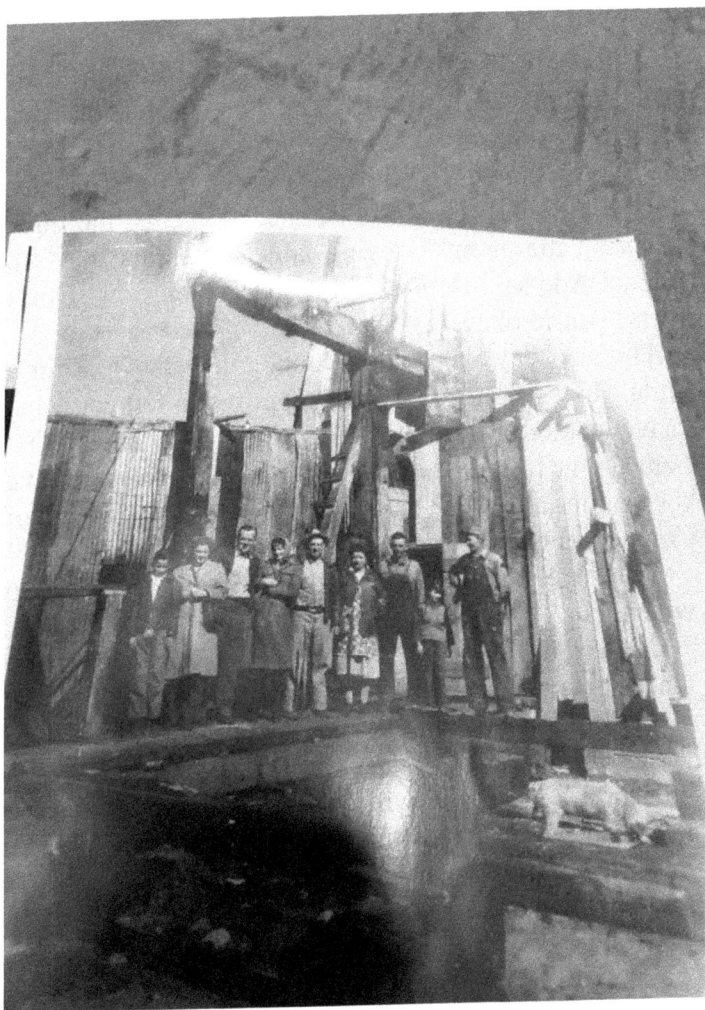

Charles A. Lindbergh Jr., on the far right at work.

I REMEMBER

1953 to 1956 - John Deere Planter Works, Moline, Illinois

Lt. Colonel Ade soon after told me the day the FBI special agents were to visit. On their arrival, the two passed by me and seated themselves to talk with Colonel Ade. The meeting continued for some time. Then Lt. Colonel Ade left with the FBI special agents, the three observing me at my drawing table. Later that day Lt. Colonel Ade said to me, "I'll be back tomorrow. Don't worry, you're okay."

The next day at lunch, Colonel Ade was silent for a while. He then said, "I am not supposed to tell you what I have learned. I'm asking you to keep quiet about what I am going to tell you. I know who you are and have known for quite some time. You're the kidnapped son of Colonel Lindbergh. You're Charles."

Tears welled up in his eyes to the point he stopped to wipe them.

He told me that the Mafia was behind the kidnap and that Alphonse Capone was involved, the bastard.

He continued, "Nothing will come out until your father dies; there's politics. The FBI has kept an eye on you for a long time. I will be long gone before you are identified. The FBI also believe you witnessed Husted, Sr., kill Miss Adele Walsh."

I agreed that I did.

He said, "We believe Don Husted, Sr., knows you're Lindbergh and is afraid of you; you know too much. Husted, Sr., is going to try to set you up for a fall."

During this time, I learned of my brothers, Jon Lindbergh, and Land Lindbergh, who were attending Stanford University.

I also relived in my mind the killing of Ms. Welsh, which had been a highly traumatic experience.

Colonel Ade and the FBI special agents continued their communications.

In 1953, Bill Oehler promoted me to the college engineers' education program and assigned me to redesign all casting parts and allowed me freedom with the responsibility to do research. These opportunities yielded gains for John Deere Planter Works and represented to me wage increases and bonuses.

1952 to 1950 – At 509 19th Avenue, Moline, Illinois, the residence of Loren Paul Husted (aka Charlie A. Lindbergh, Jr.), Son Paul Craig Husted, and His Mother Jane "Buckman" Husted

While at John Deere Planter Works, I received a phone call from U.S. Navy Commodore Wesley W. Howe, who asked me to allow him an opportunity for him to visit me that evening. He indicated he was passing through en route to Washington, D.C. When USN Commodore Wes Howe arrived that evening, he remained less than ten minutes. He was a quiet man, dressed in a dark blue-black suit, white dress shirt, dark tie, and shined black shoes.

Wes observed my face and just sat on the couch looking at me. We made no worthwhile conversation. That was my last visit with Commodore Howe until 1998 and June 16, 1999, at 9:50 a.m. when I called Mr. Howe. At that time, he said to me, "I am interested in hearing your story," and then banged down the phone.

Wes Howe was married to Annie Juarez, an attractive Castilian Spanish girl that Husted, Sr., and his wife Helen had brought to live with them in 1944.

1956 - John Deere Planter Works, Moline Illinois

Unaware of Stockholm syndrome and not consciously comprehending in-depth my being the kidnapped son of Colonel Charles A. Lindbergh, Sr., in face of great protest from Lt. Colonel Guy Wade, from chief Engineer William P. 'Bill' Oehler, from personnel director Lloyd Rasmussen, and from John Deere Planter Works Vice President/Plant Manager John E. Hoffman not to leave John Deere Planter Works.

I terminated my employment to enter the insurance business in San Luis Obispo, California. I intended to establish a career for myself in the general insurance and life insurance business.

John Hoffman offered a wage increase of $150 monthly and other amenities.

Lt. Colonel Ade, who had the dirty work facts on Husted, Sr., pleaded with me, saying, "You're walking into a trap." The Lt. Colonel said, "Husted, Sr., has a hold on you. When a person gets beat on for a long period of time, that person becomes a prisoner. You're a prisoner of the bastard's abuses."

Through 1955-1956, Don W. Husted, Sr., vigorously pleaded I take over his insurance agency. Husted, Sr., apologized for his abuse. He told me he had less than two years to live and was going to undergo surgery for removal of polyps from his esophagus.

In 1955, Husted, Sr., provided roundtrip express bus tickets so I could assess his proposed lucrative offers.

Lt. Colonel Ade told me, "Your life is in danger."

At Tucumcari, New Mexico en route to San Luis Obispo, California, the bus driver received a phone in the message with instructions to keep me insight. The remainder of the journey, I sat front right, visiting with the bus driver.

After arriving at San Luis Obispo, California, Husted, Sr. showed me a subdivision house that he said was mine. He also evidenced a document guaranteeing a $750 per month income. I was undecided.

George Parrish, field agent for Glen Falls Fire and Casualty Company, signed me up for the Golden Gate College Insurance Course. Then after the week's visit, I returned by express bus to Moline, Illinois.

I REMEMBER

The time was March 1956 when I decided to accept the offers by Husted, Sr.

Years later, in 1983, when I had finally broken the Stockholm Syndrome, I realized how wise the perception of Lt. Colonel Guy W. Ade had been.

In early 1956, Lt. Colonel Ade briefed me, "It is evident we cannot convince you to stay with us. Please keep what I tell you confidential. Husted, Sr. is going to offer you a partnership agreement, and he will insist you buy a one hundred-thousand-dollar life insurance policy making him the beneficiary. You do so; you're dead."

The Lt. Colonel added the Husted, Sr., was a suspect in the killing of Elizabeth Short known as the Black Dahlia and who in 1947 was murdered in Leimert Park neighborhood of Los Angeles. How he knew this, I do not know, as it is also one of the most famous unsolved murders in American history.

He also said, "I think Husted, Sr., and that concubine he calls a wife, are the two who kidnapped Bobbi Greenlease. Husted, Sr. is mixed up with the Mafia."

Again, why he accused Husted, Sr., of the kidnapping of Bobby, the six-year-old son of Robert Cosgrove Greenlease Sr., a multi-millionaire automobile dealer, I do not have a clue. As far as I know from the news is that Bobby was murdered by Bonnie Emily Brown Heady and Carl Austin.

On May 6, 1956, I entered the general insurance and life insurance business. Less than four months into the insurance business, Husted, Sr. presented me with a partnership agreement and life insurance application for $100,000. I burst into a haughty laugh and said to Husted, Sr., "I will agree on one condition, we buy one hundred-thousand-dollar policy on your life and make me the beneficiary."

Husted Sr. heatedly declined, and I said no to his proposal.

Soon I received a call from James M. Ketchie, general agent, from The Canada Life Assurance Company in San Jose, California. Jim tried to sell me on accepting the offer, but I firmly replied, "No!"

I called Lt. Colonel Ade and said, "Colonel, I apologize for not accepting your advice," and conveyed to him that Husted, Sr., had not kept his offers.

Lt. Colonel Ade told me to hang in, to stay independent, and to consult, if necessary, with the FBI in San Francisco, California.

On declining the partnership and life insurance policy, troubled waters soon followed. I had launched my marketing plan in the *San Luis Obispo Telegram-Tribune* and directed letters to local merchants. I began my work at 7:00 a.m., or earlier. I had power of attorney to underwriting performance and completion bonds and, on bond letting days, would be at the contractor's bid auction at 5:00 a.m. to 6:00 a.m.

By Christmas, I owned thirty contractor accounts. By late 1957, I owned two-thirds of all downtown merchant accounts and commercial accounts south into Santa Maria, California, northwest into Morrow Bay, California, and northeast into Santa Margarita and Atascadero, California.

The combined education afforded me at John Deere Planter Works, the Alexander Hamilton Institute for Business & Finance, the Golden Gate College Insurance curriculum, my youth on the street selling papers, washing windows, and my spirit to survive, all afforded me a will to grow in wisdom in the face of troubled waters.

As a youth in San Luis Obispo, after delivering my paper route, I would sell more papers on the street downtown. One of my customers was Harry Takken, a shoe cobbler, who instead of putting new soles on my shoes for $2.75, had me stand on a box and guided me through the paces of reworking the soles and heels of my well-worn shoes at a cost of fifty cents.

"Someday," he once said to me, "you could make a good shoe cobbler, maybe work for me."

Then he gave me a $10.00 bill and welcomed me to return to learn more, which I occasionally did.

Upon entering the insurance business, Mr. Takken gave me all his insurance lines. He told me the Aetna risk analysis would get me lots of business. I was never certain what insurance I had.

My writings and life depict my quality relations with merchants, judges, and interesting colorful situations. To some, I was humorously called Charlie or Charles.

I was also a threat to Husted, Sr., and to certain competitors who lost thousands of premium dollars. I was also a threat to the Husted, Sr.'s brothers, Don W. Husted, Jr., and Richard Lee Husted. They feared me by virtue of their envy and the bad influence exerted by their father and stepmother, Helen.

Among San Luis Obispo, California insurance brokers, I was one of a few who owned a complete fire & Casualty Surety Bond and Life and Insurance supplemented library, according to W. B. "Barney" Brandt.

KEVIN HUSTED, SR.

On July 8, 1956, at 8:10 p.m., I was working up new commercial accounts in Aetna surveys. Richard Lee Husted and Don W. Husted, Jr. appeared at the glass door entrance of my office. I unlocked the door, courteously greeted the two as I seated to continue my organization and assessment of client policy coverages. I said, "What can I do for you men?"

Husted, Jr. replied, "Our father does not like your ideas. He told you not to advertise in the newspapers; we are going to kill you."

The two swept my desk clean. Books, policies, and papers flew around the office. They jumped up on the desk and pushed me backward in my chair to the floor. A calm presence of mind and strength, by the grace of God, provided the ability to put a vise grip hold on the two and pull them facedown to the desk.

With the wrist arm hold on Richard, I pinned him face down onto the hard floor. While doing this, Don, Jr. broke my grip, ran to the restroom, and returned with a jagged coke bottle he had broken on the washbasin. When he lunged toward me, I grabbed his wrist upward and the jugged Coke bottle fell from his hand. I pressed Don, Jr. to the deck again, and held the two in a locked position. Richard began to cry, and Don, Jr. apologized, and soon the two were on their way out the door.

I reported their violent attack to the police. My autobiography describes many rough, dangerous situations, including corruption, embezzlement, false claims, and efforts to peg me on missing funds. Three longtime general insurance brokers, who had lost substantial premium, offered me opportunities in their Brokerage operations. Alec Madonna, owner of

Madonna Construction and Madonna Inn offered to finance my buying out Don Wesley Husted, Sr.

In October 1960, I sold my book of business to Husted, Sr., he paid $2000 down and never paid the balance.

THE MAFIA OATH

1956 - W.B. "Brandt, Vice President, Sayre & Toso, Inc., San Francisco, California

I have never been suspicious of people. God endowed me with nerves like the finest steel, keen intuition, and the ability to synthesize. When a paperboy delivering my route and selling papers along Higuera Street and Monterey Street, I encountered many people including some who were bookies and the sheriff who was taking payoffs on cockfights. I delivered papers to a house of ill repute, and one day vowed I would return as an FBI special agent and effect a cleanup, a boyhood dream. To me, entering the insurance business meant that one day, I would use my agency to front for the FBI.

On occasion, I would visit Red Corcoran's Coffee Shop to relive in my mind my being taken by Mr. Simon to visit with the FBI special agent Jim Haman and my father, Colonel Lindbergh, Sr., and my visit on the street just outside Red Corcoran's Coffee Shop. I would also visit Austin's and relive the encounter of the two visitors in front of the spigots; Jim Haman and my father, Colonel Lindbergh.

On one occasion, I conversed with Judge Ray B. Lyon (Stanford Graduate). One Sunday afternoon, when I was a lad, the judge had met me at the back entrance to the jail. We visited his chambers; the judge had me strip to my shorts to view my battered body, neck, and face. Then, I dressed and sat in a chair. The judge called me "Son," while he made a telephone call to Husted, Sr.

At that time, Judge Lyon used hard profanity and threats demanding Husted, Sr. to be in his chambers Monday at 8:00 a.m. The judge and I had been long-time friends along with traffic Judge Paul Jackson, a blind man. The two judges placed their homeowner's policies with my companies.

Husted, Sr., was disliked by many downtown merchants, except the corrupt, and some who had done time in prison including Richard Ferzzetting, Bert Bertonoli, and Virgil Negranti who were some of his clients.

Husted, Sr., had an attorney, Martin Polin, Esq. Husted, Sr. who showed me evidence of me still being followed, as he did in 1943. He was innately desperate to prevent being caught for his killings and robbery of the Bank of America in Cambrian Pines, California. Husted, Sr., was desperate to the measure he had since 1939 continuously attempted to destroy my credibility.

Prior to Thanksgiving 1956, I received a phone call from W.B. Brandt, who told me he represented Sayre and Toso, Inc., San Francisco, California. Mr. Brandt declined to meet at my office in the Anchor Insurance and Realty Building owned by Husted, Sr.

KEVIN HUSTED, SR.

Instead, he introduced me to petrale at a steak and seafood restaurant on the south end of San Luis Obispo, California. Mr. Brandt told me he had served with A.P. Giannini on the Bank of Italy Board of Directors. Mr. Brandt gave me direction on a policy few brokers presented to their clients. He said, "You will generate new merchant clients by presenting the U and O policy," (Use and Occupancy). Mr. Brandt told me Husted, Sr., "Is out to hurt you in business, and I suggest you move from his building. Several of the big brokers would like you to join their firms."

I preferred to build up a book, then sell out and move to a larger city. I selected the New Hampshire Fire & Casualty U&O policy, which had provisions that out measured other insurance carriers. I put the U&O to the test resulting in a continuous flow of new business up through October 1960.

Mr. Brandt was a distinguished gentleman, coarse face, and hands wore a Masonic ring, calm, patient, thorough, precise, and made his point clear. He wore steel gray and black navy-blue suit, white shirts, conservative ties, black socks, and well-shined black shoes.

On one occasion, I asked Mr. Brandt if he had ever met FBI Director J. Edgar Hoover, but I received no reply.

His four-door black Mercedes Benz was well kept.

Often Mr. Brandt called for a lunch appointment, and through each interview I learned valued ideas, one being the application of the U&O policy and another that in less than four decades a continued education curriculum would be a requirement of the California State

Department of Insurance. Mr. Brandt educated me on Sayre & Toso, Inc., brokerage policies underwritten by Lloyd's of London.

Mr. Brandt told me that Sayre & Toso, Inc., asked if I would work the aviation and professional markets marketing their Capital Disability policy with the mysterious disappearance provision. In a short time, I yielded a substantial book of an aviation business, which included the Greyhound Flying Club (total of eleven aircraft), a Howard powered by a 475 hp Pratt Whitney engine, several race cars, and an Aero Commander owned by Alec Madonna.

There were crashes, one killing six passengers. My autography illustrates the successes, the corruption, and my ability to endure. I did not realize in this time frame of May 1956 and October 1960 that I was being framed, set up by Reverend Don W. Husted, Sr., James M. Ketchie, attorney Martin Polin, and a consortium of FBI special agents and their Mafia affiliates. I came to this knowledge in 1967.

Prior to Thanksgiving 1960, Mr. Brandt called to have me consider a brokerage offer in Sacramento, California. Mr. Brandt invited me to visit Sayre & Toso, Inc., San Francisco, California, and Sayre & Toso, Inc., put me up in the Hotel Whitcomb.

The next morning, I met with Mr. Brandt at Sayre and Toso, Inc. We waited for Mr. Cochella who called prior to noon telling Mr. Brandt he would not be keeping the appointment and asked to speak with me. Coachella and I set an appointment at his Forum Building office in Sacramento, California. Mr. Brandt and I had lunch at his favorite restaurant, Tadich Grill, where we lunched on petrale.

On another visit, we dined in the basement alley Domino Club. That evening I returned to San Luis Obispo, California.

The next day I confirmed my appointment with Mr. Cochella, a week ahead, allowing time to clean up details on client business. Flying PSA to Sacramento, California from the Paso Robles Airport, I took an evening flight into Sacramento. Mr. Cochella told me, "My chauffeur knows what you look like and will be waiting."

With briefcase and a suitcase in my hands, the chauffeur, who had a yellow cab, met me, and spoke with a hoarse voice. For certain, he knew who I was as we crossed over the steel-girder bridge into Sacramento.

On the drive to the meeting, another driver sideswiped us two or three times and sped on ahead.

The Sicilian appearing character laughed. I asked, "Why don't you turn the character over to the highway patrol?"

He replied, "This happens all the time. You just stay on the road, keep moving."

The chauffeur drove me to the Hotel Manor. Marge Judd, Mr. Cochella's secretary, had reserved a quality room for me there.

The next morning, I walked several blocks to the Forum Building, to the second-floor suite of Frank A. Coachella – headquarters for National Home Underwriters. I peered through the second-floor windows onto the street when a well- kept Lincoln, four-door, white trim on black, pulled up, and the same chauffeur emerged. He opened the rear door and out stepped. Mr. Cochella.

By noon, Mr. Cochella and I were dining at the Parkview Restaurant in the judge's chambers dining room. We stopped at the bar where Mi. Coachella bought drinks, vodka for himself, and I had orange juice. Mr. Cochella ordered steak and recommended the mahi; I selected petrale.

Mr. Coachella carried on in a rough voice, saying, "I know all about you. I know who you really are; you will find out one day. You're very brilliant. You could be my son-in-law. My daughter should fall in love with you. One day, you will carry on what I have built. I treat you like my son. I tell you, you ever double-cross me, I cut your throat," as he pointed the steak knife at me. "You stay with me; you'll be wealthy. No one will ever give you trouble."

Mr. Cochella told me he had connections with the Air Force. "I own the vacant land adjacent to Aerojet. Look, I need your decision within the week."

"Mr. Cochella, it would take at least thirty days. I'm booked and must keep up my cash flow."

Mr. Cochella then said, "I'll call Husted; he will buy you out."

That afternoon Mr. Cochella introduced me to Tommy Chan, owner of General Produce.

The next day Mr. Cochella introduced me to Dr. Prizenzanna, M.D. who worked at the Provenzano Clinic. He took me to lunch at the Pheasant Club. Mr. Cochella related to me that Dr. Prizenzanna does all of his employees' physical examinations.

We set an appointment for my return, and I took a PSA Morning flight to Paso Robles California. Onboard the flight, I talked to a contractor who told me he owned a concrete pipe company.

I returned to Sacramento, California in my new Volvo fastback with a cruise speed of 110 mph. The Mercedes front suspension design made driving easy. In Sacramento, I checked in at the Hotel Manor.

After arriving to meet Mr. Cochella, we lunched at Frank Fat known for the Chinese bartender and their famous 17 oz. T- bone steaks.

In the course of a week, I met state senators, congressmen, and the Insurance Commissioner.

Mr. Cochella even suggested to me, "If you would like a beautiful ass, I can arrange it. I drink, gamble and play. I don't expect you to do as I do. I will be introducing you to my daughter."

I gave no response, so Frank forced a decision. At a lunch at the Parkview Restaurant, wisdom told me, Frank was a sly fox, cunning, and sinister. Yet, I was curious to learn more and agreed to a lot of ample time to assess the opportunity Frank afforded.

Tommy Chan and his family were planning the opening day of 'SEE' (Sacramento Employee Enterprise), the first discount house in California. Frank provided me a Xerox business projection; forty years hence, by the year 2000, discount conglomerates will dominate consumer buying forcing out big-name stores.

Frank Cochella assigned me to organize a Farmers Insurance Agency in place at 'SEE.' I did so, and on opening day weekend, substantial premiums were realized. Frank said, "You and I are going to do well."

I REMEMBER

As we walked a few blocks to the Wells Fargo Bank, he proudly stated, "I'm on the board. You will be ensuring borrowers for their loan amount. You must use my companies."

Frank introduced me to Wells Fargo Bank executives.

We then walked to the office of Ken Farmer, general agent for Connecticut General Life Insurance Co. Frank told Ken Farmer to provide me membership in the Optimist Club and the Toastmaster Club. I attended several meetings and made my first impromptu speech at the Toastmaster Club.

Frank opened doors to economic and social activities, and I knew well how to work the opportunities to his benefit, to the consumer, and to the benefit of my own economics.

Frank and I were chauffeured in his white on black Lincoln sedan to the Forum Building from the Pheasant Club. As Frank and I approached the building, Frank was calm, well-groomed, well dressed, and relaxed in his dark suit, white shirt, and conservative tie. I carried my briefcase.

Inside the lobby, his chauffeur pushed the button, and we stepped into a dim amber lighted elevator. I positioned myself in the center with my back to the light. Frank was on my left and to our right front the chauffeur was at the elevator operation panel.

The elevator door shut. Frank conversed in Italian with the ruddy appearing character. The elevator moved, Frank spoke in Italian, and a down number two could be seen. Frank clutched my left wrist, pulled my arm straight, and pricked his finger and mine. As Frank pressed our fingers together, Frank demanded I repeat after him in Italian and directed the operator to move to my side.

I repeated the Mafia Cosa Nostra oath as I watched the fresh blood splatter onto the elevator floor and on my shoes.

Then Frank took a crumpled piece of paper from the operator man, pressed the paper into my cupped hand, and lit the paper with a cigarette lighter. As the paper flamed, Frank and I completed the oath. Frank let my wrist loose. After the ashes fell, in his coarse voice, Frank said to me, "When you grow up, you will understand, and you will come to know your real name.

Frank then addressed Joe and said, "You are the witness."

I turned right to view the elevator operator. Frank introduced us saying, "Joe is my bodyguard."

When we shook hands, I noticed that Joe had a shoulder holster and revolver. The elevator moved to the second-floor entrance.

I walked to my desk, searching for answers, and recalled years earlier the Cotanneo cousins' refrain, "Lindbergh, when you grow up, we will pull you into the Mafia."

The forced Mafia oath was followed by Melvin Judd inviting me to fish at the landfill pond on the property adjacent to Aerojet. My intuition sensed death. On the pond bank in this desolate area, Melvin Judd and I were visited by the elevator operator who had come on us. I am certain Mel Judd was a party to the Coachella dirt works. I said to him, "This is no place for me, there are no fish in the pond. I'll find my way back." Mr. Judd packed up his fishing gear and drove me to the Hotel Manor.

Coachella's secretary, Marge Judd, sent a message early in the morning for me to call. That morning, I walked to the Forum Building Office. Marge Judd asked me to visit a Milton Berger, owner of Berger Sales, in the office of Dr. Prisenzanno. Marge related that Wells Fargo Bank would not release loan monies to Mr. Berger until there was proof of life insurance in force. Marge said, "Frank and Dr. Prisenzanno are waiting for you and Mr. Berger."

Marge Judd then called Mr. Berger and told him I was en route. When I met Mr. Berger, I was gazing at a real heavyweight, 300 pounds. My new Volvo sedan tilted as I pulled up to the barred fence at the Provenzano clinic, then the gate rolled open. I saw Frank in the examination room. Mr. Berge precisely weighed 315 pounds, although the second part of his application indicated 250 pounds.

Frank put his finger on the signature line and told me to sign and handed me a commission check payable to me for $2,756. "Frank, I can't sign this."

"You're like my son, sign it!"

"Frank, to sign this is in violation of the insurance code, a misdemeanor. In the event Mr. Berger dies, a coroner's report would evidence his true weight, and the insurance company could deny paying the face amount. Sorry I'm not into fraud; no, Frank."

Still demanding I sign, he said to me, "I control the Insurance Commissioner. I run this city."

"Mr. Cochella, you do not run me."

"No," Frank continued to yell. "This check is yours. Just sign it. You're wet behind the ears."

As he grew more furious, I replied, "Frank, no, shove this black pen and check up your ass. I operate a clean business; you and I are through."

I exited the Provenzano Clinic, the tall wrought-iron gate rolled open, and I traveled to the Forum Building Coachella office to clean out my desk. The staff ignored me.

Marge Judd told me, "You made a big mistake."

In a side office, I called the FBI. FBI special agent Sanborn listened as I conveyed this recent activity.

Special agent Sanborn said to me, "If you have problems, give me a call."

There was another intimidation in the time frame of the forced Mafia oath.

1959 – October - 698 March Street, San Luis Obispo, California, Office of Anchor Real Estate, an Insurance Agency Owned by Reverend Don W. Husted, Sr., and Leased Office of Loren Paul Husted (Charles A. Lindbergh, Jr.)

It was mid-afternoon when I arrived at my Marsh street insurance agency office. Joanne Thrall was the agency secretary; her husband was a U.S. Navy pilot. On entering the office, Husted, Sr. called his associate James M. Ketchie, general agent with The Canada Life Assurance Company in San Jose, California. Then Husted, Sr. went into a tantrum as he paced the floor screaming and calling me names. "You have ruined everything. You have screwed up the works. Ketchie and

I will break you." As he ranted, his nostrils flared like a snorting bull.

James M. Ketchie called and spoke to me. He was furious and demanded I meet him at an abandoned A & W Root Beer stand off Highway 101, South of Atascadero, California.

Jim Ketchie and I met at midmorning, and I asked him, "Jim, what is the big shakeup?" I was seated in his new salmon-colored Chrysler Imperial.

On closing the passenger door, Jim Ketchie tossed a tantrum, spun his tires skidding left and right, blasting gravel and dirt before hitting solid traction on the blacktop side road and racing onto 101 North at speeds more than 100 miles per hour. Continuously spouting a stream of profanity, he threatened to blackball my business career. He said, "You have ruined our plans, you screwed up the works. You're stupid."

Still going at high speed, Ketchie pulled into the abandoned A& W root beer stand, and the car once more began to skid. I was neither rattled nor frightened.

I exited his vehicle, and as I entered my Volvo sedan, I observed Ketchie speeding spinning in the gravel and turning north on 101.

Upon arriving at my office, I calmly and firmly said to Husted, Sr., "I am selling my book of business to one of the local insurance brokers, or you can sell your book of business to me."

"I have the backing to buy you out." Husted, Sr., went bonkers.

Secretary Joanne Chrall was visibly trembling.

I then tested his warped conscience. I said, "I believe you manipulated the scheme to plant me in the Coachella operations to cover your heinous crimes. You and Jim Ketchie are playing G-man with the FBI. Downtown the word is you want me out of the way. Alec Madonna has offered to finance my buying you out; the word is you're moving to San Jose, California. You son of a bitch, the day will come when I send you to prison for killing Adele Welsh. Tell me why in 1935, 1936, your mother, Myrtle Husted said, 'This is not Paul, this boy has a cowlick? I'm calling the police.' You and your father threatened to lock her up. I'm calling Coachella to let him know I think you and Ketchie are snoops."

"We will kill you," Husted, Sr., said.

I continued to deliberately chide Husted, Sr. in front of Joanne Chrall at a distance of twenty feet from where he stood in the doorway to his private office. His color changed from pasty white to beet red to white; his nostrils spread. At one point, he wildly shook his fist at me.

The dirty works escalated. Often in the morning, I found my tires flat, and the lug nuts screwed loose.

During the night, frequent anonymous phone calls woke me abruptly from sleep. Many incidents of this nature happened between 1956-1960.

Neither James M. Ketchie nor Don W. Husted, Sr. ever evidenced knowing that I was negotiating with Frank A. Coachella prior to my declining to join the Coachella operation. Following their erratic behavior, I called Frank A. Coachella and disclosed that Husted, Sr. and Ketchie had angrily informed me that I had screwed up their plans.

Mr. Cochella replied, "Someone tried to plant you in my operation. If you ever need help, call me."

Husted, Sr. demanded I release my book of client accounts to him, and James M. Ketchie owed me $5,000 in commissions. A second call to Mr. Cochella resulted in him calling Husted, Sr. and Ketchie. J.M. Ketchie lost his promotion to being Vice President of The Canada Life Assurance Company, Toronto, Canada.

1959 - San Luis Obispo, California

In the time prior to attempting to position me with Frank A. Coachella, Reverend Don Wesley Husted, Sr., engaged in conservation with USMC Captain John Buckman. The two discussed Attorney Robert L. Mezzetti as their contact.

Once, I eavesdropped on Reverend Don Wesley Husted, Sr., James M. Ketchie, and Attorney Charlie Black, who discussed a plan to communicate with the FBI on supposed Mafia Families in Santa Clara Valley, California.

At one point, I traveled with Reverend Don Wesley Husted, Sr., to the residence of an FBI special agent who was en route to Puerto Rico, or so Husted, Sr. led me to believe. I am certain, beyond a shadow of a doubt, that Husted, Sr. feared his mother, Myrtle, and myself, which accounts for the continuous verbal cutting comments he directed towards his mother to her demise and his constant effort to discredit my character.

THE GARDEN PATCH

1959 - At the One-Acre Garden Patch of John Franklin "Frank" Loveland, El Dorado, Kansas

In 1959 toward the end of October, I had cleaned up all client details, collected commissions, changed grant deeds on three parcels, packed up all our belongings into a tandem axle U-Haul trailer, and moved my wife, Jane, and son to Wichita, Kansas.

We located a comfortable duplex and had moved in shortly before Thanksgiving.

I then began a serious search of the facts leading to my being the Lindbergh boy. I first visited with Frankie Loveland Tarrant, sister of Viola Mae Hoggett Husted, and a stepdaughter of Frank Loveland. Frankie and Viola were the sisters of Katie Sigman.

Frankie told me, "I best keep my trap shut. Viola says for me to stay away from Charlie Sigman unless I want to get myself killed. Charlie is mean."

I bid her goodbye and walked to the field to visit Frank, who was spading the soil.

I REMEMBER

At age 84, Frank was known for being a peaceful, kind man, who had for years worked the soil with horse-drawn equipment. He had never driven a powered vehicle or equipment and was known to read the Bible daily.

Before I could inquire, Frank told me, "I am eight-four, not too many years left. You should know who you are, how you got here, you're a Lindbergh. You should go ask Charlie Sigman; he knows who you are. That's all I can tell you. Charlie is dangerous."

I assured Frank of my silence. We visited a short time and talked about the hamburger stand his wife once owned.

I walked back to the house and asked Viola if she would go with me to visit Sigman, but she declined.

I traveled alone to the Sigman Farmhouse. At the bunkhouse kitchen, a nurse directed me to the tenant house where Katie was caring for Willie Louise.

I had parked my auto outbound on the far side of the tar-covered parking area. As I passed the double low sill windows, I could see Willie Louise Sigman.

The nightstand was crowded with medicine bottles. Willie was fat and swollen. I stepped up, knocked, and Katie let me in telling me, "Willie is bedfast."

I stopped several feet inside the door, and suddenly Willie went hysterical. "My God, my God, mother, we are all going to prison."

Katie told Willie to hush, saying, "He doesn't know. Your father will kill us."

Then Katie demanded I leave and pushed me through the door.

I walked to the front entrance of the big farmhouse, and after looking down the cistern, where years earlier I had dumped frogs, Charlie yelled for me to come in.

Sitting in a rocker, I could see he was not in too good health as he had for years chewed Red Man Tobacco and spat in a spittoon.

The front room was trashed with paper and stored items.

I asked how I could be of help. I recalled the time in 1951 when we had visited with Harry Truman by phone about my draft status and my U.S. Navy Reserve status. My call had irritated Truman, and I then called on General LaMay and General Shaffer.

Almost abruptly, I quickly inquired of Charlie Sigman to tell me what happened years ago, how did I get here, and why Willie Louis would go hysterical saying, "We are all going to prison."

Charlie became unglued, swung his cane at me, cursed me, and said to me, "It's not for you to know. Get out now. If you want to stay alive, get out, and never come back to Wichita, Kansas."

My Divorce

In the 1959 to 1960-time frame, my divorce from Jane Buckman Husted was finalized.

I married Kay in Ft Worth, Texas. We traveled by train to San Jose, California, to rear Brad and Craig, my son by Jane Buckman Husted. This move was intended to be a valuable new start forward. It was the beginning of years of grief.

I REMEMBER

1959 – October, Wichita, Kansas

I had joined Northwestern Mutual Life Insurance Company and soon discovered I was blacklisted through Retail Credit Company, now Equifax, Inc. I made the connection in Milwaukee, Wisconsin, where cryptomnesia memory blooms lofted by the strong Italian people I had met. I asked for directions to the Italian section of Milwaukee and soon found myself walking into Little Italy on the waterfront area. With ease and comfort, searching faces, I suddenly discovered I was being followed by a well-dressed man attired was a dark suit, black shoes, white shirt, and dark tie.

My roommate was an older man whose attire was a dark suit, black shoes, black socks, white shirt conservative tie, and he was non-committal. This gentleman and several insurance agents invited me to dine at Nino's, an Italian Restaurant famous for T- bone steaks. Though I produced well, word came out that I was not Northwestern agent material according to a report out of San Luis, Obispo, California.

So, I joined the Sheldon Anderson New York Life Insurance Agency, a $21,000,000 annual volume firm not counting the two major players, Elmer Moore and Bob Norton, whose combined production exceeded $70,000,000.

Sheldon Anderson made me untouchable by the Equifax Inc. report out of San Luis Obispo, California. Agile, with keen ability to comprehend, in less than forty seconds after learning a parable, I canned the book by William Danforth, *I DARE YOU* and went on to be Salesman of the Month for three straight months. I was also enlisted to train low volume producers on cold call solicitation of new prospective clients. The then unexplained mystic of intuition, discernment, and perception current since a lad enabled me to discover a crime in the office.

When I joined this agency, Sheldon Anderson, general agent, New York Life Insurance Company, Wichita, Kansas, provided me a tour of all the departments. On meeting the controller, wisdom told me that this man had been embezzling monies.

Sheldon Anderson and I discussed my hunch, but no more was said. Some months later, the controller was arrested for stealing $17,000.

Anderson also received calls from Reverend Don W. Husted, Sr., and anonymous phone calls too.

When Anderson failed to terminate my Nylic contract, Husted, Sr. had Robert L. Mezzetti wrote a letter to Mr. Anderson and the Kansas State Department of Insurance.

Later, Anderson told me, "You're okay here. But you have real enemies."

Arriving a few days later, Reverend Don W. Husted, Sr. held a closed-door session with my boss, Sheldon Anderson, who did not like Husted Sr.'s stories about me. Husted, Sr. characterized me as an unfit father, a thief of the fund, a homosexual, and an all-around bad guy. I sued my wife, Jane Buckman Husted, for divorce (infidelity), and custody of my son, Craig, and filed charges of insanity for violent assaults against me.

Husted, Sr. had Attorney Robert L. Mezzetti write a damaging letter to my attorney and the presiding Judge.

Anderson Nylic, the manager, assured my attorney and Judge Lamb that Husted, Sr. and Mezzetti were attempting to blacklist me. The court favored me, and I was of good reputation.

The Judge granted me custody of my son, Craig.

Extending My Education

An FBI special agent had visited Sheldon Anderson.

This gave me the opportunity to enroll in a program held at the Lassen Hotel, an education, and coaching in public relations workshop that was a takeoff on the Dale Carnegie Institute. The attendance was sparse and included Rich Pond, son of Chief of Police, Wichita, Kansas, three FBI special agents, a person with Occidental Petroleum, and the son of Reverend Art Wilson. After seven evening sessions, the FBI special agents no longer attended.

KEVIN HUSTED, SR.

THE HOME WAS MANY PLACES

1935 - At 241 South Volutsia street, Wichita Kansas, Residence of Loren McFadden Husted, and Wife Myrtle Husted.

I arrived following the birth of Don Wesley Husted, Jr. The day I arrived, there were fireworks and sparklers, which formed my basis for declaring I arrived on July 4, 1935.

In 1935 through 1944, it was during this time frame Don Wesley Husted, Jr., his brother Richard Lee Husted, their sister Judy Sharon Husted, resided with their parents Reverend Don Wesley Husted, Sr., and wife Viola Mae Husted.

From 1935-1944 I resided an estimated sixty-five percent of this nine-year time frame with Loren and Myrtle Husted and the balance of the time with Reverend Don W. Husted, Sr., his wife, Viola, with Charles S. "Charlie" Sigman, his wife, Kate, and with Fred and Ida Pepperdine. The estimated 5.85 years residing in and out of the care of Loren and Myrtle were valued days of establishing Biblical values.

I REMEMBER

FBI records evidence the date of my visit to Wichita, Kansas FBI office.

1954 - Moline, Illinois - On Leave From the USMC

Don Wesley Husted, Jr. stopped to visit me in my residence. While there, he poured Clorox in my drinking water. On smelling it, I demanded he leave my house.

1956 - San Luis Obispo, California

Don Wesley Husted, Jr., went to our Johnson Avenue duplex, shaved off my son's hair, and Richard burned a two-inch cigarette scar on my newly finished drum table. Woodworking is my hobby; I had worked out seven finishes on the drum table.

1956 to May 1959 - October, San Luis Obispo, California

In this time frame, I generated many commercial accounts, uncovered fraud activity, embezzlement, and endured horrific situations caused by Reverend Don Wesley Husted, Sr., his wife, and Don Wesley Husted, Jr.

Many nights were haunted by me receiving deep breathing threatening anonymous phone calls. My tires were slashed, and the lug nuts loosened.

The immorality within the Baptist Church on Pismo Street led by Husted, Sr. was likened to Sodom and Gomorrah, in my opinion. For the sake of my young son, Craig, I tolerated his mother. She shocked me. I returned home from Sacramento, California, to find her naked in bed in an embrace with another woman, Helen Nye. Helen Nye was one of my many lesbian friends and a member of the church.

Immediately after this distasteful episode, I filed for divorce and culminated it while I was in Wichita, Kansas.

1967 - Hamilton Avenue, San Jose, California

Don Wesley Husted, Jr. paid us a surprise visit bringing gifts for my wife Kay from Egypt. His conversation was laced with obscene words. I demanded he not use obscene language in the presence of my family. He burst into a rage, saying to me, "You will soon be dead, I will fuck your wife and raise your son."

I calmly opened the door, and with a vice grip on his wrist, rolled him through the door.

1970 - Sierra Avenue Residence, San Jose California

One day, Don Wesley Husted, Jr. entered our residence through the rear utility room without knocking. First, he grabbed an iron, yelling in a rage, swung it at me, struck me with a glancing blow across my brow drawing blood. With my arms and hands, I covered my head. He then attempted to strangle me with a cord.

My son, Brad, ran to the phone to call the police, but Don Jr. grabbed him, saying, "If you call the police, I'll kill your father and you."

It was then I wrestled Don Jr. out to the front porch. I reported the assault to the FBI. Knowing that the San

Jose, California police were in on the blacklist of me, I avoided filing a police report.

1978 - Croft Rental Company

I was looking for storage space. Unknown to me, Don W. Husted, Jr. was moving his goods into a storage area in the same hallway. "I've got something for you," he said.

Then at the storage door entrance, he attempted to shove me inside. Being agile, I moved the door and Husted, Jr. With my heart pounding, I ran from the area.

1978 - Berryessa Flea Market

Reverend Don Wesley Husted, Sr., and Don, Jr. influenced my former wife, Kay, for a long time. Since early childhood, my son Kevin had evidenced robust diligence to work and generate income.

In 1978, Don Wesley Husted, Jr. exerted his influence on Kay to allow Kevin to work weekends selling his junk at the Flea Market. I opposed this, of course, but Kay insisted. I finally consented, providing that I accompany Kevin. Don reluctantly accepted this arrangement. Throughout the day, Don exhibited weird behavior, mumbling about killing someone, telling Kevin, "Sell, or you don't get paid."

At day's end, I sat in the center of his truck and placed Kevin on the passenger side. On Highway 17 in Campbell, CA, an estimated one mile before the Hamilton Avenue access, from his left jacket pocket Husted, Jr. suddenly brandished a. 32 caliber automatic.

I immediately caught his wrist and pulled his arm forward and down to the floorboard as we were rapidly moving down the freeway.

Husted, Jr. began to rant and rave. My vice grip on his wrist, however, finally caused the handgun to fall to the floorboard, and with my left foot, I kicked the gun under the seat. Kevin then grasped the top of the steering wheel and wisely steered the truck to the ice plant just past the Hamilton access.

I switched off the ignition and threw the keys to the passenger floorboard. Husted, Jr., could not recover his right arm due to my hold on his left arm held near the floorboard.

Making sure we were well into the ice plant, and out of the stream of traffic, Kevin opened the passenger door.

I then told Kevin to move up to the access road. When Kevin was a considerable distance away, I broke free of Husted, Jr., who was now folded into the steering wheel. When Kevin and I crossed over the freeway Hamilton Avenue overpass, Husted Jr. was still in his truck on the ice plant. Kevin was never paid; Don Wesley Husted, Jr., and his father were well known for failing to pay their employees.

1982 – Adele Welsh Murder

In 1982 Reverend Don Wesley Husted, Sr. during a visit with Sgt. Donald J. Zies and me, discussed my being a witness to the March 1, 1941 slaying of Adele Welsh by Reverend Don Wesley Husted, Sr. in Kansas City, Missouri. In our visit, I answered questions over the telephone directed by a homicide detective from the Kansas City, Missouri police department. A short time later, I called Reverend Don Wesley Husted, Sr., at his marriage counselor's office, in the Cathedral of Faith Church, San Jose, California. I told Husted, Sr. that local and Missouri authorities were going to place him on trial for the March 1, 1941 slaying of Adele Welsh. I said, "I am their witness."

Husted, Sr., went into a rage, telling me he would crush my neck and would kill me when he found me.

I cut him short and said, "Hey, first, you have to find me."

Husted, Sr., met with his attorney, Robert L. Mezzetti, and son Don Wesley Husted, Jr., who influenced him to back off from causing me any covert trouble. Allegedly they advised that I was tough and that I would fight back.

Don Wesley Husted, Jr., called later and told me that he was personally responsible for their backing off from causing me trouble and said, "I told him he best leave you alone."

1984 - Winchester Blvd., San Jose, California

I visited the residence of my son Kevin and his wife, Susan. It was early evening when I arrived. Susan Woolery called asking my son, Kevin, to assist in cooperating with her, Reverend Don Wesley Husted, Sr., and the police in locking me in a mental hospital.

Kevin cut short her conversation.

Very soon, we discovered that Sasha Woolery, Susan's sister, was in communication with the police department of San Jose, California, in addition to FBI Agent Jim Page, FBI Agent Malcolm B. "Buck" Sample, and FBI Agent Adrian D. Coulter.

1944 – The Bank Robbery

In 1944, at the First National Bank, 1111 Chorro Street, San Luis Obispo, California, Reverend Donald W. Husted, Sr., and James M. Ketchie opened a business partnership working out of a cubicle side office in the bank. Jim Ketchie joined the Canada Life Company, and Husted, Sr., began Anchor Real Estate and Insurance.

I was a silent young lad growing up, an innate listener (a skill I have learned to appreciate).

It was during this time frame that my father, Colonel Charles A. Lindbergh, observed me at Red Cochrane's Coffee Shop, and again with Jim Hanan at Austin's at the soda fountain.

The two met at the bank vault location close to their office. Shortly after their conversation, Reverend Don Wesley Husted, Sr., took me on a gunpoint robbery of the Bank of America in Cambrian Pines, California. James M. Ketchie and Reverend Don Wesley Husted, Sr., used to discuss my being the Lindbergh boy.

On a late afternoon, Jim Ketchie told me, "When you're of legal age, I will bring you into my business." Jim also told me he wanted me to meet his friends. He drove me to the country sagebrush area of Baywood Park, California.

We dined with his friends. One was a well-known psychic. She told Jim that evening that I was the kidnapped Lindbergh boy.

113

I REMEMBER

1956 – James M. Ketchie

1956, May 4th, James M. Ketchie kept his 1944 promise, and contracted me to The Canada Life Assurance Company, Aetna Fire, and Casualty, and educated me well in commercial insurance risk analysis. During this time, Jim Ketchie and his wife Willie entertained me at their comfortable Husted Avenue, San Jose, CA residence. On the second visit, I was their guest at the De Anza Hotel and first to swim in their new swimming pool. At their residence, I become acquainted with their daughters, Pamela and Dianne. We enjoyed their lighted oval pool.

In the kitchen, Jim and Willie discussed my being the Lindbergh boy, and something about Stanford University. Jim Ketchie put me through weeks of education and an anti-stress course.

Between 1956 and 1959, I did underwrite many commercial accounts for clients, and an estimated eight to ten of those were for Italian-Sicilian figures. From the McMillian Mortgage Co., I bought 150 construction policies for new houses. I owned the finest quality major medical insurance policies, $2000 per month disability income insurance and $500,000 term life insurance payable to my son Craig. I tolerated my wife, Jane, out of mercy for my son Craig.

For me, the years 1956 – 1959 were packed with financial success and the discovery of corruption. The blowout with Frank A. Coachella and James M. Ketchie was the beginning of tough times. While eavesdropping on Husted, Sr., and USMC Captain John Buckman, I first learned of attorney Robert L. Mezzetti.

KEVIN HUSTED, SR.

October – 1961, November

My wife, Kay, our sons, Brad, Craig, and I arrived from Newton, Kansas, a German Mennonite township northeast of Wichita, Kansas, in San Jose, California. My Kansas attorney, Milton Zachariah, advised that we move from Wichita, Kansas. After Kansas Judge Lamb had granted me an unrestricted custody decree, Kay and I decided to establish our residence in San Jose, California. A factor in this decision was to collect the $20,000 balance owed from the 1959 sale of my book of business to Reverend Don Wesley Husted, Sr., San Luis Obispo, California.

Our arrival sent Reverend Don Wesley Husted, Sr., into a rage. He told me his Attorney, Bob Mezzetti, and District Attorney Louis Bergna would make sure I would never build a business or have a job. "You're done, you, your family, will beg in the streets; you're done, you're finished," he threatened.

I ignored his threats with no consideration of his ability to carry out a blacklist.

1960 - Valley Christian School

My wife, Kay, and I went to enter our sons, Brad and Craig, in Valley Christian. I was well educated on the value of Christian schooling in San Luis Obispo, California, and from 1956 – 1959, I had placed insurance coverage on three Christian schools. The director and staff at Valley Christian School said to us, "You, your wife, and sons are not fit to mix with our members; we know all about you. You're no good!"

I replied, "Tell me what you know; the fact is, you could know nothing. We are good parents; our sons are good kids. It sounds like you know Reverend Don Wesley Husted, Sr., his attorney Bob Mezzetti, District Attorney Louis Bergna, and FBI Agent Jim Page. Are you aware that Reverend Husted, Sr. is a murderer?"

The director and attending staff burst in anger. The director asked us to leave. We enrolled our sons in a public school.

On reading the Kansas custody decree, the principal, Mr. Hoyt, told us he would store the enrollment files at his residence to protect us from being located.

"Mr. Curry would like to visit with you, your wife Kay, and your sons."

1961 - Forrest J. Curry, General Agent, The Penn Mutual Life Insurance Co.

I applied through the San Jose, California sub-general agent B. Michael Anderson, CLU, Wichita, Kansas. New York Life insurance Co. General agent, Sheldon B. Anderson, provided a valued character and production report to B. Michael Anderson. I initially attended the Curry Agency education curriculum program. Three weeks into the program Mike Anderson told me, "I have terrible information on you from the Retail Credit Inspection Company and General Manager James H. Strobridge. Mr. Curry would like to visit with you, your wife Kay, and your sons."

In the Forest J. Curry Agency office, the Curry secretary cared for our sons Brad and Craig. Kay and I visited with Mr. Curry, who paused, observed Kay, myself, and then told us as he held up a thick report, "I am a good judge of character, and this terrible report does not fit you two. I do not believe this report."

I then asked to read the report, but Mr. Curry said, "The Retail Credit Company will not allow us to disclose the content of inspection reports and information sources."

I replied, "Mr. Curry, the characterization and the false information could be the work of District Attorney Luis Bergna, Attorney Bob Mezzetti, FBI Agent Jim Page and Reverend Don Wesley Husted, Sr."

Mr. Curry nodded, and said, "Yes, but how did you know?"

He stood and pulled a $100 bill from his pocket and said, "This is for your time, and we're going to lunch at the German Haufbrau." He then added, "The phone call I took was from my secretary. She told me that she had received two anonymous phone calls, one a man, one a woman, and said their comments were terrible. I am putting a copy of this report in our fire safe. I have to return the original report to the Retail Credit Company."

Over lunch, we visited in close proximity in order to be heard over the noise.

Mr. Curry said to Kay and me, "They are making your husband out to be a whacko and saying that he should be put away!"

The report was unbelievable. Mr. Curry paid our cab fare to the train depot. Kay was a "hang-in" lady; we traveled home and began anew.

I REMEMBER

1961- Electrolux Company

Harold Jacobson, sales manager, and I went into sales training. Two weeks later and several sales at an early morning sales meeting, Mr. Jacobson called me into his office, told me he had to terminate my employment. He said that District Attorney Louis Bergna called and told him that I was bad. He said, "I am told not to trust you, and to terminate you."

I received a commission check and moved on.

District Attorney Louis Bergna repeated the blacklist activity at Kirby Company and at Grolier Company. The general agent for Guardian Life Insurance Company set me up and then terminated my contract telling me he was a friend of District Attorney Louis Bergna.

1961 - Christmas Time

During Christmas time, FBI Agent C.D. 'Moose' Marron told me that I was not in trouble with the FBI. He said, "Iowa authorities have a kidnap warrant in the Sheriff's Warrant Department; your Kansas custody decree has jurisdiction. The Iowa warrant is invalid. Private detective Steve Bowman is en route from Wichita, Kansas to kidnap you and your son, Craig. Tell your wife to call me if you or your son are picked up. The FBI will arrest Bowman on kidnapping. You should move your family. I've no regard for Don Husted. He has disclosed your location to Steve Bowman and is assisting your former wife, Jane, and her father to set aside your Kansas custody decree. When Steve Bowman shows up, call me."

118

KEVIN HUSTED, SR.

FBI Agent Moose Marron told me, "I know you well going back many years. You're okay. The Sheriff Warrant Officer has pigeonholed the warrant."

Several days passed, but suddenly, I observed a Kansas license plate on the car north of our residence. I called Wichita, Kansas, Chief of Police. The chief provided the information that the vehicle belonged to Steve Bowman. "We have no warrant for you. The Iowa warrant is invalid; I have a copy of the Kansas custody decree. I have visited with Mr. Marron."

I then called FBI Agent Moose Marron and the Sheriff Warrant Officer, who told me he had personally related to Steve Bowman that his warrant documents were invalid.

Next, Don Wesley Husted, Sr., called to say, "You're going to prison, you're going to lose Craig."

He informed me that Steve Bowman was staying at the Starlight Motel on Stevens Creek Boulevard.

I replied, "FBI Agent Moose Marron assures me the Iowa warrant is invalid and the Kansas custody decree has jurisdiction."

Husted, Sr., said, "I'll fix you with the FBI."

I then called Detective Steve Bowman at the Starlight Motel, Room 31. It was late at night. "Mr. Bowman, FBI Agent Moose Marron tells me the Iowa warrant is invalid, and you will be cited for kidnapping if you take my son and me. In very short minutes, a friend and I will be at your door to have you arrested for attempted kidnapping and flaunting false documents."

After this conversation, I drove over to the motel with a friend. When we arrived, Steve Bowman had vacated, not to be heard from again.

The communication with FBI Agent Moose created a kindred attitude. I was welcomed at his office and on a visit disclosed to FBI Agent Moose Marron the sordid Retail Credit Inspection Company report and blacklisting by District Attorney Louis Bergna, Attorney Bob Mezzetti, Don Husted, Sr., and FBI Agent Jim Page.

Mr. Marron assured me he would acquire the Retail Inspection Report. He did so but would not disclose to me the contents.

FBI Agent Moose Marron influenced Harvard Business School Graduate Ernest D. Hazeltine, CEO General Agent of the Mutual Benefit Life Insurance Company, to contact me as a broker agent and to include me in his educational curriculum.

In those few months before November 1961, I did well. I generated one client, Bill Purdy, owner of the Purdy Plumbing Company – a commission of $4000 – to be paid in November.

It was morning. I sat outside the office of Mr. Hazeltine, studying the insurance curriculum. Hazeltine was in a conference with Michael B. Orr, his agency education manager. When I went into his office, Hazeltine told Michael Orr that FBI Agent Moose believes Paul is the Lindbergh boy. He then suggested to Orr, "Call your father at Weyerhaeuser in Seattle, Washington. He knows Colonel Lindbergh. Ask your father to come down."

The senior Orr visited. It was apparent he was observing me as we sat through several days of education sessions.

Hazeltine then hosted a cocktail party at the Stanford University Club.

Through the evening, my wife Kay and I were the personal guests of Mr. and Mrs. Percey. At that time, Mr. Percey was CEO of The Mutual Benefit Life Insurance Company.

This potential recognition of my Lindbergh identity was a boost to Kay, and our sons and me during the 1961 last quarter. On the other side, Reverend Don Wesley Husted, Sr., and Attorney Robert Mezzetti and Attorney Dunn (representing my first wife, Jane), had succeeded before Judge Peckham to affect a writ of habeas corpus and to not honor the Kansas custody decree.

Previously, we had been protected by Judge Salzman, who scolded Attorney Mezzetti, Attorney Dunn, and Reverend Don Wesley Husted, Sr., for their dirty work in taking Craig away from me.

Judge Salzman had support from FBI Agent Moose Marron who would do as he damned well pleased with no concern to whoever did or did not like it. Judge Salzman was moved up the judicial bench and to another area. Judge Peckham presided over the case previously presided over by Judge Salzman.

On request of my son, Craig, to not let the court send him back to Kansas to his mother, we went undercover. I violated the writ and kept in phone communications with the Sheriff Warrant Chief, who had pigeonholed the warrant. The pressure was put on the Sheriff Warrant Chief by Attorney Dunn, Reverend Don W. Husted, Sr., and Attorney Robert L. Mezzetti. Moving undercover meant a change of public school, but the new school principal would not coverup the records and our address.

Daily I walked our sons to school. On the morning of 1961 November 1, I was cautious. On Halloween night, a terrible hunch told me I would lose my son. For the last time, I packed my son's lunch, kneeled, prayed, and then I walked Craig into the school building.

At home, I prepared to go to the Hazeltine Agency, but my car would not start. The rotor had been removed.

Reverend Don Wesley, Husted, Sr., arrived at our door.

Kay and I were traumatized. Husted, Sr., told me we must talk.

I said, "Since you know where we live, and you want to talk, you can drive me to my office building parking lot."

As I ascended the stairs, I sensed being observed. Turning right, 180 degrees, I then saw an unmarked car and driver.

Mr. Hazeltine was in his Stanford office. I picked up a commission check, descended the stairs, and entered the Husted, Sr., five-star Pontiac. Instantly I heard the screech of wheels as the unmarked cars closed in front, rear, and side. Sheriff Deputy Steve DiMiel, known well to Sgt. Don Sizes, tapped on the window and asked me to get out. Motioning, he said, "I must take you in on this warrant."

I replied, "Be patient when I finish opening my mail, I will go with you."

Husted, Sr., was hilarious, telling me that I was going to put you away for many years. "You will never see Craig again."

I retorted, "The day will arrive when I send you to prison for killing Adel Welsh."

Sheriff Deputy Steve DiMiel cuffed me. En route to the Country Jail, Deputy DiMiel told me they had no choice. "Husted, Sr. set you up. If I could turn you free, I would. I am telling the Judge you're a gentleman."

It was then I learned that Sheriff Deputy Salzman was the son of Judge Salzman.

I was booked into jail and taken to the second floor. The desk sergeant told me they had words that I was not a bad guy. "FBI Agent Marron is your friend. During the day, you can stay with us; you eat with us," he said as he poured me a cup of black coffee. "You can make your calls from this phone. You're being railroaded; I suggest you call the Governor."

The PBX operator then put in an emergency call to Governor Pat Brown who listened and then told me he would connect me with Cecil Poole. Mr. Poole listened, and that morning called FBI Special Agent Moose Marron.

The desk sergeant that morning told me Judge Peckham would call for my release once my son was in flight for Kansas. That was mid-morning.

Then in 1961, Thursday, November 2, I traveled in a van from jail to court. The van was parked on the First Street driveway at the rear door of Superior Court. To my left, on the second floor, I could see FBI Agent Moose Marron who gave me a kind salute.

On the grassy area along the driveway stood Reverend Don Wesley Husted, Sr., Attorney Robert L. Mezzetti, District Attorney Louis Bergna, FBI Agent Jim Page, and a few others. They laughed, and Husted, Sr., said, "There goes the jailbird. Hey, jailbird!"

I shrugged off their haughty laughter. Not so today, thirty-nine years later, I would like to send them to hard labor in Siberia far from the beauty and the freedom of America.

On the third evening, I was released. When incarcerated, Jesuit priest Father Turney visited me, and he gave me a pack of Lucky Strikes cigarettes. I walked up the ramp to find my wife Kay, my son Brad and Husted, Sr.

First, I greeted Kay and Brad. Then I told Husted, Sr., "I will take this case to the State Supreme Court and begin the investigation of you killing Adele Welsh, Husted, Sr. went bonkers, threatened to kill me and to put me in state prison.

"For what, you son of a bitch?" I sarcastically asked.

He threatened to frame me. I assured him I would visit Frank A. Coachella in Sacramento, California, put the Mafia on his back, and blacklist Judge Peckham, which I did.

My wife Kay and I at that time moved into a house owned by Pettis H. "Hugh" Fine, a painter of houses and director of the John Birch Society. I calmly briefed Hugh Fine of the closure and loss of my son Craig. I used a cover name for my phone, and utilities with the name of Sigman. We lived there comfortably for many weeks.

I began to sell Britannica books.

While incarcerated, Husted, Sr., had stolen my $4000 commission check.

I never returned to The Hazeltine Agency.

Hugh Fine visited me. During our conversations, I made the comment, "Mr. Fine, I must find Joe Cerrito in Chicago, Illinois. Mr. Cerrito can get my son back. He can stop my being blacklisted by District Attorney Louis Bergna."

Hugh Fine then asked me, "How do you know Joe Cerrito?"

I replied, "I just know him; I don't know. It was a long time ago."

At that point, Hugh Fine told me Joe Cerrito was right here in Los Gatos, California. He said, "My father and Joe are friends. We painted all his houses. I can talk to Joe."

Hugh Fine told me he was also a friend of Louis Bergna since grade school. "Louis wouldn't hurt anyone."

"Mr. Fine, Louis Bergna has been causing me to be out of work since October 1960."

"Hey, there is something wrong, I will talk to Louis."

Days passed before Hugh Fine stopped by for a visit. At that time, he told me, "You have enemies. Tell me about this bastard Husted, Sr. Who is he? Louis Bergna tells me I should kick you out of my house. To stay you will have to join The John Birch Society."

I declined to join.

Hugh Fine then told me that I should find out who I really was, meaning the Lindbergh boy.

More days passed when Hugh Fine called and commanded me to join the John Birch Society. His voice resonated indifference. He demanded that I make threatening anonymous phone calls to the director of the psychiatric clinic to demand the release of Major General Edwin A. Walker, who the Pentagon had incarcerated for speaking out on some issues.

I calmly declined, telling Hugh Fine, "I am not going to make any threating anonymous phone calls; if I were to call, the director would know who was calling, and that you were requesting I call."

Hugh Fine called me a Communist.

On another visit, Hugh Fine opened the garage door, and I said, "Hey, what is going on?"

Hugh Fine handed a book to me on building bombs and said, "You can build and stockpile them and put them on that wide bench."

"Mr. Fine, I am not into building bombs. I will keep the book."

That afternoon I visited FBI Agent Moose Marron, who accepted my memo on the solicitations by Hugh Fine. FBI Agent Moose Marron advised me he would tell me when I should cut off Mr. Fine at the same time as when I would return the bomb book.

I attended several John Birch meetings. Hugh Fine became sociable over coffee. He told me about my father, Colonel Charles A. Lindbergh, his flight in the Sirus to Moscow. He also informed me, "Lindbergh is a Communist."

Soon, Hugh Fine called inviting me to dine on his wife's tasty cuisine. He told me, "You have been selected by four of my friends to join in a patriotic endeavor."

I joined Hugh Fine in his big kitchen; his wife's cuisine was very good. Hugh Fine again told me I had been selected to be the fifth man in a plot to assassinate President Kennedy.

Several dinners passed and unknown to Hugh Fine, I edited and forwarded to FBI Agent Moose Marron his solicitation to assassinate President Kennedy. Hugh Fine demanded I join the four characters, and I requested to meet the four men.

Hugh Fine told me, "You will meet them when you decide to assist in the plot to assassinate President Kennedy."

FBI Agent Moose Marron told me, "Mail Hugh Fine the bomb book and tell him you are not one to kill the President and you have disclosed the scheme to the FBI."

I did so. I related to Hugh Fine, "I am not given to killing people, and for certain, not President Kennedy. Fact is, you and District Attorney Louis Bergna Contrived this illegal felony entrapment. I will be talking to Frank Coachella about you and Louis Bergna."

Hugh Fine went off the wall. He doubled our rent and cut off our utilities.

It took the PG&E CEO in San Francisco, California, to restore services. The local PG&E manager was a John Birch member and friend of Lois Bergna.

I paid no rent, and we took six months to move. We faced harassment by characters driving unmarked cars and by Reverend Don Wesley Husted, Sr. Friends of Husted, Sr. rammed our Hillman Minx auto, shearing the flat camshaft and the Sheriff Civil Division repossessed our broken-down car and sold it for $56.57.

On foot, I walked many a mile selling whatever products I could sell. Husted, Sr., would drive by in his new Pontiac five star, laughing at me.

A day or two passed, and I received a typed letter from Husted, Sr., telling me I looked shabby, have holes in my shoe soles, and that I needed a haircut. He wrote, "Your car is gone, your son is gone, and your wife is a whore." He even told me I was in this condition because I did not trust in Jesus.

This was a person who owed me $24,000.

A Break for Lindbergh, Jr., and Family

My wife Kay and I found new friends, Edith and Grace Millard, heirs to Strathmore Packing and friends of FBI Agent C.D. "Moose" Marron. The sisters invested $25,000 in Charles Simon's sleep teach institute courses; the inventory filled 2/3 of a bedroom.

The sisters had paid the cost of a year's lease on a prime store space in Mayfield Mall, and they offered me 85% of the gross sales of inventory. We bumped up the retail price and set a per person enrollment fee per seminar session.

I edited a ten-page book on a global setting, desire, and motivation.

The sisters ran an ad in the newspaper, and we sent letters to real estate firms, firms with salesmen, the Orowheat Company, and Helwig Nut, and Bolts.

At the first evening seminar, there were twenty-five men and women enrolled at ten dollars each; courses were sold.

Stone & Schultz Realty requested a seminar for their sales staff. No one showed. I received a haughty call scoffing our seminar and the course curriculum.

I discovered days later that Husted, Sr., and Attorney Bob Mezzetti were thick with Don Stone and Lou Schultz.

The Milliard sisters sent Husted, Sr., on his way when he attempted to blacklist me, again. The sisters were close friends to Superior Court Judge Hall. They had earlier written off their investment as a loss and my organization and zeal resulted in a 15% gain of their total loss.

In this time frame of late 1961 through early 1963, the Millard sisters told me, "We believe you're the Charles Lindbergh who was kidnapped. Mr. Marron also believes you are."

The sisters brought in a well-known psychic. This lady confirmed as well that I was Lindbergh, but there were politics involved. Edith and Grace Millard encouraged me to take my birth name back.

My son Kevin was born on May 22, 1962. In June, Edith Millard called me and told me that Mr. Marron had asked me to visit the FBI office. She said, "I will drive you; bring Kay, and your sons to rest at our house."

June Millard's house was air-conditioned. Bless her heart; now I can see Kay, Brad, and Kevin, in this New York pram, sitting in the cool of the air conditioning as Edith Millard and I go through the front door to her new Buick sedan.

We traveled to the FBI office in the St. James Post Office and went through the second-floor entrance.

FBI Agent Moose Marron seated Edith Milliard to my left backside. Mr. Marron motioned me to visit with a tall character attired in summer tan cloth. FBI Agent Moose Marron positioned himself at the door entrance to his office, his right arm overhead. Moose is a giant of a man 6'7" and affable.

FBI Agent Connally was seated at the First Street desk, on the phone discussing Cascade properties.

An FBI agent seated to the right faced the wall, pecking on a typewriter.

I stepped to the counter table and greeted FBI Agent Sample. I experienced a sudden calm, serenity; we were seated across from each other and began to visit. "I told Mr. Sample, "You're Charles Sample, Charles A. Sample."

His eyes were somber and awesome. The FBI agent pecking on the typewriter stopped and turned 180 degrees to look at FBI Agent Moose Marron. FBI Agent Connolly dismissed his phone call, looked at me, and then looked at FBI Agent Moose Marron.

These reactions were in the same second that the FBI Agent Moose Marron swung his right arm down to his right leg, did a 360-degree spin, and said, "I knew it, I knew it, he is the Lindbergh boy."

FBI Agent Connally went, "Sheesh."

FBI Agent Sample wrote on a small piece of paper, "Charles A. Sample, FBI Agent," an address and a phone number.

We stood.

FBI Agent Sample said, "Write me often; write to me all that you know, tell me everything."

We parted. Some years later, I discovered Charles A. Sample to be FBI Agent Malcolm B. 'Buck' Sample, criminologist.

Shortly after this encounter with the FBI, a person by the name of Christiansen gave me an old Datsun sedan. It had a clean white exterior and interior in the trunk.

I carried a five-gallon can of sump oil and a funnel since a drive to the summit in the Santa Cruz Mountains necessitated two quarts of oil.

KEVIN HUSTED, SR.

FBI Agent Moose Marron influenced Julian Kitchin, education manager with the James D. Rosezell General Agency, for the New England Life Insurance Company to grant me a producing agents' contact.

My office time was spent in the office of Julian Kitchin, age 71, a Christian Scientist. Mr. Kitchin suggested that I work directly with him and to avoid Rosezell, mentioning that "for some reason, he doesn't like you."

In the closed office of Julian Kitchin, Julian would discuss the Atlantic flight of Colonel Lindbergh, the poetry of Anne Lindbergh, Alphonse Capone, and that the Mafia owned Brookdale Lodge in Felton, CA.

On occasion, in this time frame, the Millard sisters would also discuss Sam Miano and Alphonse Capone.

I was frequently a guest for lunch at their residence in Scotts Valley, California. Julian had brief telephone visits with Sam Miano in Capitol, California.

I was assigned to service orphan policies on supposed Mafia figures. My wife Kay and I were guests at the Rosezell Christmas party and dinner.

Friends of District Attorney Louis Bergna, two men named Ray Bronson and Jim Jensen, made big conversation on gliders and a planned hinterland visit to Cuernavaca, Mexico.

Julian Kitchin arranged with Watsonville, California Chevrolet dealer David Hart for me to buy a used Ford two-door sedan. En route to picking up the Ford, the oil-burning Datsun burned out. I walked to Watsonville from the Santa Cruz, California access.

James D. Rosezell opened with an Agency Golf Tournament. I had been assigned to partner with Julian

Kitchin. Mr. Kitchin said to me, "You and I will start late; we arrive late."

In the office, Mr. Kitchin told me that on the third hole, "we will be joined by Sam Miano. You must trail behind; you're not to talk with him or come near where we walk."

On the third hole, Sam Miano joined Julian Kitchin, dressed in a black baggy suit, a wide-brim black hat, brim turned down, and coat with the collar up around his face. Kitchin and Miano walked and talked in a low voice.

My psyche clicked at the base of my neck; I picked up a sense of being shot dead.

Prior to the fourth hole, Sam Miano walked off, right to the road.

Julian Kitchin and I played out the course.

In my 1939, 1940, and 1956 doodles, I frequently sketched Sam Miano in detail fishing on the Chicago, Illinois shoreline, but in 1956, Husted, Sr. stole my finest sketch of him.

Louis Bergna again resurfaced to make frequent false charges against me to James D. Rosezell. In this time frame, I frequently discovered that FBI Agent Moose Marron followed me in his white two-door auto. Witness testimony and FBI records evidence the covert observation and 'head games.'

I generated an $11,000 commission on a rated twenty-five pay life policy. Jack Cooper, the client, was rated Table F. James D. Rosezell told me the New England Life rate was not acceptable and had me place the issue through a Pat Lernihan who stole the commission. I sued and lost.

Witnesses to the scam involving District Attorney Louis Bergna and James D. Rosezell are Henning Moe, Jim Jensen, Louis Bergna, Ray Bronson, and my wife.

My wife and I moved to Nevin Way, San Jose, CA just weeks before the assassination of President John F. Kennedy.

The Lenihans and James D. Rosezell also caused measures of grief during that period. I uncovered the fact that District Attorney Louis Bergna was trashing my diligent efforts to generate income. These individuals made our 1963 Christmas tough. Father and son Joseph and Patrick Lernihan relayed to me that Joe Cerrito would kill my sons and me if I didn't back off on collecting the $11,000. A colorful scene occurred when I wore a trench coat and carried a black umbrella. The temperature was cold; heavy rain fell when I visited Joe Cerrito Lincoln, Mercury dealership, now located in New Gatos, California DMV office.

Joe Cerrito had his bodyguard let me in. Mr. Cerrito was calm and quiet, a man of few words. I succinctly conveyed to Mr. Cerrito the threats, adding, "Mr. Cerrito, it is not my business that you may or may not be a Mafia Don, but is it true you would kill my sons and I for my action to collect my eleven thousand dollar commission check?"

Mr. Cerrito assured me in a few words that he would not kill my sons or me. "You go," he said, "I'll tend to this problem."

James D. Rosezell, and the Lernihans could not handle my direct complaint to Joseph Cerrito. I collected $250 of the $11,000 commission. In court, the Lernihans evidenced no assets, according to my representing attorney Harold Rauch.

At our Nevin Way residence, we faced harassment by the Retail Credit Inspection Company and Sgt. Kirby with the Office of the District Attorney.

FBI Agent Moose Marron ran a DMV license plate on Sgt. Kirby and discovered he was with the Retail Credit Inspection Company. FBI Agent Moose Marron then gave me a copy of his police rap sheet; he was a felon with a two-page crime record.

Bethel Assembly of God Church, San Jose, CA

My wife Kay, my sons, and I attended Bethel the Hope of My Heart Church to have a church home for Kay, Brad, and Kevin. Reverend Leland Keyes was not too kind of a person. We would soon learn that FBI Agent Jim Page and Reverend Don Wesley Husted, Sr., were prominent, affluent members in the Christian Business's Association and attended Bethel Church. I was not aware that the church membership was heavy with authorities from the Office of the District Attorney, San Jose Police Department, the Office of the Sheriff, and Italian, Sicilian families.

The 1964 to 1965 years consisted mostly of the raw story that drove us away from church people for a while and an occasional evening visit to St. Joseph Catholic Church.

KEVIN HUSTED, SR.

1965 - Harold "Hal" Hampson General Agent – Mutual Trust Life Insurance Co., Willow Glen, San Jose, CA

Hal Hampson, a Bethel member, invited me to join his agency. Within weeks, I had earned a conference qualification to visit Lucerne, Switzerland.

John Crotty, Vice President of the Mutual Trust Life Insurance Company, visited the agency. Mr. Crotty and I visited for several hours, and he told me that he and his parents had been neighbors to Alphonse Capone. He and the Capone children were escorted to school in Capone's bulletproof brown on the brown limousine.

At the school, a Capone henchman would stand guard throughout the day.

Mr. Crotty recounted the late-night silence occasionally interrupted with machinegun fire.

Cryptomnesia bloomed; I asked Mr. Crotty if he had even been to the Iwen Reis Pipe Shop?

He got excited, and said, "Yes," and then told me to go on. Our visit was interrupted by a person from the Retail Credit Inspection Company.

Mr. Crotty further told me he was looking forward to seeing more of my wife and me in Lucerne, Switzerland. "We are having a meeting on you now, as a matter of fact," he added.

Hal Hampson stepped from his office and invited me into his office with Mr. Crotty. The individuals from Retail Credit Inspection Company told Mr. Crotty they would interview by phone with District Attorney Louis Bergna. Hal Hampson then asked me to leave the office, and to be sure I locked the door telling me to be there in the morning.

The next morning when I arrived, Hal Hampson told me to clean out my desk and never return. "Mr. Crotty and I were there hours on the phone with Louis Bergna. Perhaps you didn't know, Louis Bergna and I are longtime friends."

The commission loss was critical. My calls to John Crotty were rejected.

1966 AND BEYOND

My wife Kay, our sons Brad and Kevin, and I looked for a house. I am one given to editing my goals and desire and strategies. I assumed at 4 ¼% a $22,500 mortgage for a four-bedroom, shake roof house on a quarter of an acre on Cherry Lane, Saratoga, CA. The yard was landscaped with a Bing and a Royal Anne cherry tree and a bamboo arbor. A house owner some miles away gave us eighteen rosebushes. Kevin was four at the time when Brad, Kevin, and I dug up and planted the rosebushes.

I received a call from WT 'Woody' Thornhill, a general agent for the Maccabees Mutual Life Insurance Company. Woody Thornhill said, "I am opening a door for you; come to my office."

Following the Hampson Agency blacklist, I visited District Attorney Louis Bergna. Arriving in his office, I noticed his assistant DA standing to his right. The two wore loaded shoulder holsters. I asked, "What is your problem? Tell me why you're causing us grief?"

The two gave a haughty laugh, and Bergna told me to get out!

My wife Kay was ecstatic. We settled into our comfortable house when the cherry trees were in bloom. I had plowed under the yard, turned out the soil and sown seed. We turned the bamboo arbor into a gazebo.

All utilities and the phone were in the name of Charles S. Sigman. Our neighbors knew us as such.

I signed agent production contracts with Woody Thornhill and in less than five days generated commissions of $876. A few days passed until the Thornhill's secretary, a middle-aged woman, informed me that I must speak to her.

My first and only policy client was Mr. Massey, a Police Detective. I sensed no threat.

Days turned into weeks. Woody Thornhill continuously told me the check was on its way. I delivered the policy.

Our monthly mortgage payment went past due. By phone, Woody Thornhill finally told me the check was in. On arriving, I noticed his office door closed. In hushed tones, the secretary said, "Please don't get me fired. From the beginning, Mr. Thornhill, Don Husted, Sr., and District Attorney Louis Bergna have schemed to break you down."

In the office were Don Husted, Sr., Mr. Thornhill, and Mr. Roberts. I calmly entered. Husted, Sr. was sitting in Mr. Thornhill's chair. Mr. Roberts and Thornhill were reading and laughing over the Retail Credit Inspection report. The three passed it back and forth. Thornhill held up my check telling me I could not have the check. I firmly asked to see the report. The three roared with laughter.

Thornhill then told me, "You didn't know Reverend Husted, and I are longtime friends. We set you up. You, your wife, your children will beg in the street."

I replied, "You will pay for this."

En route to my car, I was stopped by a retired life insurance agent, name unknown. He said to me, "I know what is going on; you should go to the Labor Commission and file for your commissions under the wage and commission law."

I did so.

Woody Thornhill was served the next day. The secretary called me at home, telling me that Mr. Thornhill and Don Husted, Sr. were all cooperating with District Attorney Louis Bergna and the Retail Credit Inspection Manager, James H. Strobridge to break me down.

Deputy Gurney was the presiding Labor Law Judge. I arrived early and discovered Woody Thornhill visiting with a Deputy District Attorney who became excited about my arrival. Soon to arrive, was the secretary. We entered the closed labor wage commission court. We took the oath, and Judge Gurney asked me to tell why the commission was owed to me. He then asked Mr. Thornhill to answer why he had not paid the commission.

Thornhill said, "Paul is a bad guy. You should talk to Don Husted, Sr. and the District Attorney."

The Judge told Mr. Thornhill to pay the commission, at which point he began to yell, jump up and down and bang the chair.

Judge Gurney instantly got tough, threatening to jail Thornhill and do a three-time penalty if he would not immediately sit down and be quiet. Judge Gurney then asked the middle-aged secretary if she had anything to say to why I should not be paid.

She replied, "Sir, I will probably lose my job, but I must tell the truth. My boss, Mr. Thornhill, his friend Don Husted, the District Attorney Louis Bergna, and James L. Strobridge at Retail Credit Inspection Company set up Paul to cut him down."

"In the office, I heard them discuss minding him, and his family."

Woody Thornhill went into another rage, jumping atop the chair.

Judge Gurney told Mr. Thornhill, "Sit down and write out the commission check, or I will put the cuffs on you right here and send you across the street to the jail."

The $876 check was annualized, and since I had no agent contract, Thornhill was allowed to pay the monthly as the earned commission of $73. Thornhill fired the secretary.

We lost our home.

The next morning, I called and demanded to talk with J. Edgar Hoover, Chief of the Federal Bureau of Investigation.

FBI Agent Hull accepted my call. I calmly said to Mr. Hull, "You tell Mr. Hoover to put an end to the blacklist I am facing, or I will run their blood in the street."

1960 to 1999 - Thomas Salciccia, Esq. A Valued Witness

Thomas Salciccia is a fox. His sources for information are equal to or exceed the efficiency of local authorities.

Tom is calm, patient, a listener, observant, and efficient. Tom has proven his friendship.

In 1960, Attorney Salciccia and Attorney Robert L. Mezzetti were law partners. In the time frame of 1960-1993, Attorney Mezzetti represented Reverend Don Wesley Husted, Sr., his sons, and daughter. For years Thomas Salciccia, Esq, and Sgt. Donald J. Zies, sheriff deputy had shared information on the extortion of my identity and my being Charles A. Lindbergh, Jr.

1967 to 1970

In this time frame, I consulted with Thomas Salciccia, Esq. on the extortion activity. Tom gave assistance to authorities in the FBI investigation of my identity. Individually or all together these witnesses and participants were active in the investigation and covert cover-up: Tom Salciccia, Sgt. Donald J. Zies Sgt. Stan Shaver, Sgt. Jim Arata, FBI Agent "Charles A." Malcolm B. "Buck" Sample, District Attorney Louis Bergna, FBI Agent Adrian D. Colter, and my brother, Jon M. Lindbergh.

1965 to 1970

Thomas Salciccia, Esq. received disturbing anonymous phone calls aimed at causing me grief. By limousine, Tom summoned my wife Kay to his office to discuss the anonymous calls. The substance of the anonymous calls is unknown to me.

I REMEMBER

Sgt. Donald J. Zies

July 20, 2000, Sgt. Donald J. Zies, and I visited by phone. Don told me that he and his wife had received forty-nine phone calls while they were out of town on a three-week vacation but that he had time to visit with me. I mentioned my attorney, Robert M. Damir, had retained renowned attorneys out of San Francisco, Boston, and New York. I then added, "You are going to see the FBI get a haircut.

Don Zeis said, "Hey, it's time something happened for you. After what the FBI did to you, they deserve more than a haircut. I'm on your team. I hope this happens soon. You deserve a break. This litigation has been a long time coming. Lindbergh, you were smart, you kept a square head in all situations. Keep me up to date."

"Don, my attorney will call you for an interview."

He replied, "That's okay."

In 1968, Sgt. Donald J. Zeis bought me coffee and donuts at the second-floor coffee shop at the San Jose Municipal Airport. I was not aware the plainclothes person was Don Zeis. I refer to Zeis as a man of many toupees.

A private person and unaware of cryptomnesia activity, I had full knowledge of my memories of my parents and life before and after my kidnapping that had bloomed in my mind. My calm, patient compulsive-obsessive search for my parents compelled me to visit daily the San Jose, California Airport terminal and Hyatt House lobby.

These observation posts made me an easy mark to set me up. Our conversation varied from ideas on prevention of airline hijacking to serial killers, and politics. On one occasion and just before being set up for the illegal drug blast to my brain, Sgt. Zeis asked, "If you were a judge, what punishment would you serve on a woman who had sex with her mother's Collie dog?"

I replied, "First, order the dog killed, then sentence the woman to attend church and to hard labor."

Then Sgt. Zeis pointed to the blond at the cash register and told me she is on trial for sodomy.

On other visits to the coffee shop, this frumpy blond could never look me in the eye. In the morning, I was set up for the illegal drug blast to my brain. I believed I was going to have an insurance interview. The coffee shop was closed, and as I passed the blond woman, she would not look me in the eye, nor reply to my good morning. Some years later, having met the wife of Adrian D. Coulter, I believe the blond cashier was Mrs. Coulter.

I observed Sgt. Donald J. Zies to be a no-nonsense person given to an innate skill to synthesize his perceptions. He can go undercover undiscovered by his best friend – bald or toupee – one might find him in a swimming pool under a diving board observing your ears.

Sgt. Donald J. Zies is close to his wife, his son, Marcus, his daughters, and their children.

Sgt. Zies is our friend and friend of my son, Kevin, who admitted reading critical information. This statement tells me that Sgt. Don Zies read the contrived false information and had conversations with witnesses and convert participants to the schemed covert extortion activity; to the illegal entrapments; to the illegal drug blast to my brain; to the hit contract on my life; to the

1965 to 1970 covert cover-up of my identity being Charles Augustus Lindbergh, Jr. and other contrived and false information is unknown to me.

The management of the Retail Credit Inspection Company, now Equifax, Inc., has denied me information prior to and following the Freedom of Information Act requests. Respecting the 'blue code' position of Sgt. Don Zies, I have declined to ask him to disclose the false information.

Authorities wrongfully used the contrived false information to obstruct my generating income, assets to give my family a joyful and prosperous lifestyle. Then unknown to me, contrived, erroneous witness information was totally false and unheard of in my conscience.

My reputable character is witnessed by my never allowing myself to be corrupted. Since the beginning of life in the womb, I have been single-minded, amiable, stubborn, and known to follow through on decisions. By virtue, only of our Lord's Biblical values, the precepts, the Ten Commandments, have I declined vengeance by joining in the effluent of any one European arm of covert power. My ability to employ ruthless out-management of my adversaries shall always keep me standing near the threshold that now I hold firm by my belief in our Lord Jesus Christ.

Sgt. Donald J. Zies, #1022

Would a no-nonsense character misdirect a man's path of decisions? I believe that Sgt. Zeis would not mislead anyone; to do so would be unlike him. Given Sgt. Zies to be a no-nonsense person, why would I not follow through on his encouraging stands and comments. And being a man of integrity, why would he not be the Samaritan of authority to my true identity?

I AM CHARLES A. LINDBERGH, JR.

Implications I am Charles Augustus Lindbergh, Jr. Conveyed to Sgt. Donald J. Zies

In the late 1970s, I received editorials and books on and by my parents Colonel Charles A. Lindbergh and Anne Morrow Lindbergh. On four occasions, Robert "Bob" Shattuck took my son, Kevin, and I to visit antique stores in Los Gatos and Los Altos, CA. In advance of our visit to these antique stores, Bob Shattuck would arrange with the store manager to hold the books on or about my parents for my purchase. In a Los Gatos, California antique store, Bob Shattuck introduced me to and pressed me to buy an antique red peddle car, a metal toy *Spirit of St. Louis* airplane, and a large tapestry of my father and the *Spirit of St. Louis*.

At that time, Bob Shattuck said to me, "I will ask Reeve if she will get you one of the limited issues of the Longines wristwatches bearing the inscription of the

Colonel's flight across the Atlantic." Reeve Lindbergh is my sister.

On one occasion, Ronald Orwig mailed me several magazine articles on my father and pilots of that era. Through the years I have stacked the books and magazines up to the side of my den wall and have avoided reading or scanning over them. In the course of conversations with Sgt. Donald J. Zies, we discussed the stack of books and editorials about and by my parents.

Responses in the Course of Our Conversations Made by Sgt. Donald J. Zies

- "You have gotten this far; don't stop now, you're headed in the right direction."

- "It can be very embarrassing for your siblings. You're up against big money and politics."

- At the Sheriff's office of internal affairs, Sgt. Zeis suggested to me that I should read the books. "You need to learn about your parents," he said.

- I replied, "Sergeant, when I put my book on the market, then I will read the books and magazines."

- "Jon thinks you are a reincarnation."

- "You're on the right track."

- "The FBI will probably want to hire you."

- "Just tell what they did – don't get yourself in trouble."

- "They wish this case would go away."

- "The DNA will set the situation straight."

- "Is it true the police and the FBI worked you over?"

- "They deserve their day in court."

- "Today they could not get by with what was done to you."

- "You have a good attorney, I like him; I think he can do you well; he is a fox."

- "I think you are going to come out okay."

- I said, "In the event, my siblings continue to ignore doing the DNA, my attorney will do a motion to exhume my father's body." Sgt. Zies replied, "That shot will be heard around the world."

- "My being your security advisor sounds OK to me."

- "Your siblings would be smart to unite."

- "Your story is going to send some people running for cover."

- "I think you have the story of the century."

- "I'm on your team, you're clean with us."

- "You surprised them, no one thought you would make a comeback."

- "I think your friend Vladimir has the answers to your questions."

- "Husted, Sr. was an FBI informant."

- "It sounds like Jon is running from you."

- "I am not sure why they drugged you."

- "Tom Salciccia is probably your friend."

- "They deserved to be embarrassed."

Sgt. Donald J. Zies Has Knowledge of Part or All the Hard Evidence and Has Had Conversations with Many of or With All the Witnesses and Covert Participants

Attorney Robert L. Mezzetti, Esq. is a credible unfriendly witness to and participant in the extortion of my identity. Attorney Mezzetti was a Deputy District Attorney under District Attorney Louis Bergna. Some years back, a rumor existed that he was an FBI agent. Retired FBI Agent Adrian D. Coulter would know. In my phone conversation with Adrian D. Coulter, he would often ask, "Do you know who Mezzetti is?"

I could not answer the question. In 1961 I heard Attorney Mezzetti was a member of the Cosa Nostra.

In the winter of 1959, Reverend Don Wesley Husted, Sr. was scheming with James M. Ketchie and the FBI. His role was covert spy activity on supposed Mafia families in Santa Clara County.

"Robert Mezzetti was their contact," according to USMC Captain John Buckman. A source out of Sacramento, California had told me Attorney Mezzetti was connected with Frank A. Coachella. The time is unknown to me when Attorney Mezzetti accepted to represent Reverend Don Wesley Husted, Sr, his sons, and daughter. It could have been 1959. During a courtroom performance in 1983, Attorney Mezzetti fisted a Deputy District Attorney breaking the man's nose and jaw though no legal consequences were rendered, or if there were, they were not reported in the local news media.

KEVIN HUSTED, SR.

1959 - 1960

Attorney Mezzetti directed a letter to Wichita, Kansas Judge Lamb to influence the judge against my gaining custody of my son Craig. Attorney Milton Zachariah would not allow me to read the letter. Attorney Mezzetti directed a letter to the Kansas State Department of Insurance attempting to influence the revocation of my Kansas license.

The Mezzetti files on Don Wesley Husted, Sr., his sons, and daughter, and the extortion of my identity are valued. My former wife Kay Martins Husted was witness to part, or all the extortion activity schemed and carried out by Attorney Mezzetti, District Attorney Louis Bergna, Reverend Don Wesley Husted, Sr., Don Wesley Husted, Jr., and W.T. 'Woody' Thornhill.

Don Wesley Husted, Jr., is witness to and participant in extortion activity. Several years ago, Husted, Jr. told me by phone that my son Paul Craig Husted was being influenced against me by his grandfather Buckman and Attorney Robert L. Mezzetti.

From 1954 to 1960, the attorney for Reverend Don Wesley Husted, Sr., was Martin Pollin, Esq. retired.

FBI Agent Jim Page told me, Reverend Don Wesley Husted, Sr., accepted a $100,000 payoff for my upkeeping. I specifically questioned him about my being Lindbergh and asked for his cooperation. Jim Page was abrupt and rude. Did my father Colonel Lindbergh, give in trust $100,000 to Reverend Don Wesley Husted, Sr.? The legal files of Attorney Martin Polin and Husted, Sr., would provide evidence of this transaction. FBI records may also contain evidence of this transaction along with the 1944 observation of me by my father, Colonel Charles A. Lindbergh, and FBI Agent Sherwood.

Attorney Mezzetti's and Husted, Sr.'s legal files will reveal evidence of a scheme of convert extortion activity regarding my character and identity being Charles Augustus Lindbergh, Jr. FBI records contain evidence of FBI agent participation with Reverend Don Wesley Husted, Sr., Attorney Robert L. Mezzetti, and District Attorney Louis Bergna.

Where is the trust? Where are the assets derived from the $100,000? In addition to cash from one or more bank robberies and money swindles inclusive of the $100,000 payoff to forever silence my identity.

In 1944, I recall Husted, Sr., suddenly was coming into a new car, Hart, Schaffner and Mark suits, fine furniture, and real property, and in 1956, he bought property in Santa Clara County and was building subdivisions.

Because Reverend Don Wesley Husted, Sr., had since birth been given to an incorrigible character, it would be his nature to kill, swindle, or scheme to convert FBI informant activity on supposed Mafia families to insulate his being a focus of suspicion by authorities. Current to his demise in 1993, Reverend Don Wesley Husted, Sr., continuously since 1939, defamed my character.

In 1960, I declined to join Frank A. Coachella. I also told Husted, Sr., "The day will arrive when I will send you to prison for the March 1, 1941 slaying of Ms. Adele Welsh". This intimidation tactic burst a seam in the FBI informant activity he had schemed with James M. Ketchie, FBI agent, and IRS agents.

KEVIN HUSTED, SR.

1993 to 1999 - Sgt. Jim Arata, Deputy Sheriff Retired

Jim Arata is a valued and unfriendly witness to the schemed covert extortion of my identity. Prior to my hunch, he knew about the covert cover-up and schemed drug blast to my brain. I sowed an angry seed about Attorney Bob Mezzetti in the mind of Robert E. Douglass. In less than twenty-four hours, the angry seed returned to Sgt. Jim Arata and Sgt. Donald J. Zies. I met with Sgt. Arata in a small room; he was unable to talk. On a second occasion Sgt. Jim Arata, Sgt. Zies and I met in a room. Sgt. Arata asked me what I knew about FBI Agent Coulter.

"Have you ever met FBI Agent Coulter before?"

"Yes, I think so."

Sgt. Arata appeared upset. I discerned this inquiry was pertinent to the illegal drug blast. On a third occasion, I asked Sgt. Arata if he would televise my breaking news on my being Charles A. Lindbergh, Jr.

Sgt. Arata told me that day will come soon enough. After these head games, I laid on Sgt. Jim Arata the Xtra Xtra Xtra copy regarding the kidnapping. We have not visited since. Our paths have crossed. Sgt. Jim Arata is like the rabbit on the trail; he quickly moves in the opposite direction.

FBI records and witnesses will reveal evidence of the covert participation of Sgt. Jim Arata, Deputy Sheriff, Sheriff Division, Intelligence, Office of the Sheriff, Santa Clara County, American Italian-Genovese connections with FBI and FBI Special Agent Adrian D. Coulter, and connections with Robert L. Mezzetti, Esq.

I believe that Sgt. Arata is a threat to the well-being of my son Kevin and me. Pertinent to my identity, Sgt. Arata is well short of being honest and of acting in good faith. Withholding evidence to the felony crime of kidnapping is a felony crime. The appropriate legal proceedings could turn Sgt. Arata into a valued unfriendly witness. Be it certain, Sgt. Arata is not my friend.

In 1993, Sgt. Don Zies introduced me to Sgt. Arata. My intuition called it, "Joe, you're Genovese."

This immediate recognition got to him. Intuition also told me that Sgt. Arata had the information I looked for: trap him.

Several days later I designed the Xtra Xtra Xtra memo and mailed it to my sister Reeve Lindbergh. A friend, his wife, traveling to Manila, mailed the memo from Tokyo, Japan.

Ten work days passed, I called Sgt. Jim Arata. "Sergeant Arata, did you receive the Xtra Xtra Xtra memo I wrote Reeve Lindbergh?"

"Who is this? Charles Lindbergh. You son of a bitch, where are you? I'm going to put you in jail. You're in trouble; you're kicking the lid off Pandora's Box. This could cause a problem."

"Sgt. Arata, when I'm through there will be no Pandora's box. You're going to put me in jail for telling the truth? Go for it, hotshot."

Sgt. Arata banged down the phone.

KEVIN HUSTED, SR.

1955 - Moline, Illinois.

At the John Deere Planter Works Product Design Department, Chief Engineer William P. Ochler motioned for me to accept a call on his office phone. Mr. Howe told me he was en route to Washington, DC. It was after nine p.m. when Mr. Howe arrived. Mr. Howe sat on our couch he observed me, told me briefly about his wife, Annie. I offered him a cup of coffee, but he declined. In less than ten minutes Mr. Howe departed.

Colonel Ade related to me, "I think he knows something. He wanted to see what you looked like. He is a friend of Don Husted, Sr."

My phone visit with Annie Howe in 1998 was indifferent, cold. I felt she was tense. In 1999 I called again to discuss my autobiography and Reverend Don Wesley Husted, Sr. but was cut short by Mr. Howe, who told me that he did not care to hear about my story. "Never call here again."

The 1955 visit made me believe that Mr. Howe had visited me to observe my head profile. FBI records could have recorded this visit and possibly more current communications pertinent to my autobiography.

1968 - January 8

In the months since we had lost our Saratoga, CA residence in 1967 I provided my wife, Kay, our sons Brad and Kevin, a comfortable duplex residence in Bellwood Estates, Los Gatos, California. I assumed the property at 4 ¼% on $24,500. Our Bellwood Association provided us a picnic area, sports court, a lifeguard, and a

40' x 60' pool. I covered our utilities, the phone with the name Johnny Foster – brother-in-law to Charles "Charlie" S. Sigman. We enrolled our sons in Blossom Ranch School, a private school with a garden patch, horse corral and a horse named Penny.

1970 to 1978

My wife was the underwriting secretary for the Phil San Fillipo Insurance Agency. The blacklist of my character continued. The extortionist attempted to stop Kay from joining Fireman's Fund America. In the Fireman's Fund were characters pitting Kay against me. From a *Potpourri* ad, Kay located a 19-year-old mare named Queenie. An experienced rider and member of the American Saddle Club, Kay insisted we buy Queenie. I rented a horse trailer and moved Queenie to the Santa Clara County Fairgrounds horse stables.

The winter of 1968 was cold, dipping at times into the twenties. I rented two stables, one for Queenie, and the second for saddle tack and oat/hay storage. A trucker out of Tracy, California paid me with 3 ½ tons of Canola oat hay for helping him unload his eighteen-wheel truckload of oat hay.

The saddle tack room was a place of comfort blessed with the aroma of oat hay, leather, and fresh coffee -- a place for our sons to climb, jump, nap, and enjoy over a checkered tablecloth a home-prepared picnic lunch. On our visit to the horse, we soon recognize our being observed by a retired deputy sheriff in addition to the fairground's manager, Red Lauber, and a private detective, Ly Berard, owner of Crown Detective Ly

Berard did convert work for FBI Agent Jim Page, the FBI, District Attorney Louis Bergna and Attorney Robert L. Mezzetti.

On January 8, 1968, my right femur was crushed in 90+ pieces, my right shoulder was cracked through. For situations prior to and following the accident connect with local authorities.

From ICU of Los Gatos Community Hospital, I called Moose Marron to arrange protection for my wife Kay and sons. I was confined to a Spika cast.

Reverend Don Wesley Husted Sr. visited asking me to sign a disability income application to collect $1000 per month. I declined and demanded he leave the room.

A sheriff deputy in plainclothes served me a notice to appear in court on a debt. I calmly tore up the summons in half and tossed it in the bedrail waste bag!

In 1976, I learned this same Sheriff's Deputy turned out to be a friend of Robert M. "Bob" Shattuck.

1968 – Foreclosure

I battled foreclosure proceedings from my Spika cast. We were forced to move. Three and one-half months from 1968, January 8, Dr. Paul Stewart, MD cut away the Spika cast. I walked twenty feet.

1968 - January 8 through 1968, February 13

I did isometric exercises except for my right leg in traction. In the second night of the Spika cast, I built an airflow system of surgical tubing through the open areas. My sons connected the tubes to an electric air pump under the bed with a switch on the rail. My son, Kevin, provided me a black rubber band squeezer; the frequent daily use and isometric exercises with the dynamic airflow minimized atrophy and blood pool reservoirs- and zeroed out any dizziness when the Spika cast was cut off.

The search for faces for my parents was excruciating. I inwardly hoped that my father, and my siblings would walk through the door of my hospital room, but I did not expect it. 1969 wisdom strongly told me my father was in the area or soon to arrive. I established two posts of observation the open phone booths in the municipal airport, one of which provided a view of all the passengers entering and exiting the boarding corridor, and The Hyatt House phone booth corridor provided a view of the lobby entrance and coffee shop entrance. My observations went through the day, up through dinner and into the late evening.

SEQUEL TO BRAIN BLAST

1969 - Brain Blast Short of a Lobotomy

In the municipal airport second-floor coffee shop, I paused to say hello to Lt. Stan Shaver, the deputy sheriff who had introduced me to Sgt. Donald J. Zies. I began to sit in the next booth. The agent asked me to sit on his right. This positioning placed me on the aisle. To his left was another person with black hair and a black brush mustache. We faced Lt. Stan Shaver and the backside of Sgt. Don Zies. When I paused to greet Lt. Stan Shaver, I observed my coffee cup full. Seated, I observed Lt. Stan Shaver was moving his head in line with the position of Sgt. Don Zies so I would not see his face. The agent was somber and reviewed the Life Insurance printout. I had sipped down a half of cup of coffee when a quiet, petite brunette dressed in white refilled my cup. The frumpy blonde cashier was setting up her till; the coffee shop was closed to the public.

In a few short seconds, my brain was thrust into shock. I trembled, and with simultaneous actions, I grasped the booth trim and made a fist on the table underside. In hushed tones, I began to say, "Oh Jesus, Oh Jesus, help me! Oh my God, what have you people done to me?"

I REMEMBER

The agents were somber. Lt. Stan Shaver stood up in the booth. He was laughing, he was hilarious, telling me, "You're not hurt, you're going to be okay. Visit me at my office."

Sgt. Donald J. Zies held his head in his hands.

The rush demanded I move into physical action. I let go and was in a physical fight. My car looked official; with precision skill, I accelerated to speeds in excess of ninety miles per hour. Accessing onto Highway 17, I noticed a CHP officer on his cruiser phone to my left until I turned on Stevens Creek Boulevard off Highway 17. Arriving home on McDaniel Street, I packed my suitcase telling my wife, Kay, "I am going to Washington, D.C. on business."

I packed my B2 flight navigation slide rule. Kay was baking cookies. "You're what?" she replied. "What has happened to you?"

I explained the rush.

Kay called our family physician, Doctor Michael D. Cahn, MD. I sat to speak to the doctor asking Kay for milk. I was trembling when I said, "Dr. Cahn, I have been hit by police and the Mafia. Lt. Stan Shaver is involved."

Doctor Cahn told me, "You're going to be okay. You're not hurt. The police and Mafia are not out to kill you or hurt you. I know what they're looking for. Drink down buttermilk, eat soda crackers and bread. If you have any difficulties, call me. I will prescribe 5mg Valium."

The chills and the trembling were critical. Kay covered me with a blanket. I was unable to lie down. How we got buttermilk remains a mystery. In my physical condition, I felt like I was being stunned.

Plainclothes authorities visited Kay in the foyer of our residence. I looked back over my shoulder as they huddled in conversation with Kay. None of these plainclothes officers looked me over.

Inside I prayed, concentrating to avoid falling apart.

KEVIN HUSTED, SR.

Our sons Brad and Kevin came home to see me at my worst. I struggled through an evening bath in tears, terrible traumas, and trembling. We retired, our sons and my wife soon fast asleep. Our German shepherd lay in the hallway by the door to our sons' room.

Unable to sleep, I was suddenly thrust into shock by a sudden roar and a silhouette in the space of my torso, neck, head, and a torchlight, blue flame blowing from my solar plexus through my head. I likened the blue flame thrust to a brass pump pressure blowtorch. I clung to the bed frame, and my left hand clutched the windowsill. Then the blue flame thrust, and the roar flashed out. I was exhausted, pleading the name of Jesus for help. I rose to sit and slumped exhausted to the thick rag weave rug bedside. I quietly began to crawl out of the bedroom.

As I crawled into the hallway, Kay awoke. She ran to my side. I clung to the hall carpet edges to the doorstep as I crawled down the hall. The black and white bathroom floor was cool. I slowly pulled myself up to the antique lavatory and leaned on the basin as Kay dowsed me with cold tap water. I looked into the mirror only to see a blackened skull and black holes for eyes, nose, and mouth. Fiery arrows shot from my blackened skull, and black holes for eyes sockets.

Minutes passed before the black hallucination passed, and red/blue sparks had shot from my pupils. Kay stripped me down, dried me often, dressed me in pajamas, covered me with a warm blanket, and held my right shoulder as I clung with my left hand to the molding and door sash. I sat in the Captain's Chair at the dining table. I was trembling while Kay went to the phone to call Dr. Cahn. The doctor had a modern drug courier deliver 5 mg Valium, four quarts of buttermilk, and a box of soda crackers.

Kay held the phone to my ear while I described the horrific experience and insisted this was the work of the FBI, police, and Mafia. Doctor Cahn, MD, tried to convince me the FBI, police, and Mafia were not out to kill me or hurt me. "I know what they're looking for. You're going to be okay in a few days." Doctor Cahn then recommended that I put down an occasional shot of Scotch.

I was desperate to continue the search for my parents. My lame physical condition must be made strong, I felt. The Scotch was a stimulant; the Valium gave a measure of balance to my brain. Several days passed. I called Lt. Stan Shaver to set up a visit.

When I arrived at the sheriff's office service counter, it was dark; no staff was present. In a rude manner, Lt. Shaver said, "Hey, now you know who you are; you know your real name."

I replied, "Where are my parents," then broke down in tears.

Lt. Shaver fled the area.

That evening I called Moose Marron. "Mr. Marron, why was I drugged? Lt. Stan Shaver is involved. I am in critical condition. Tell me what is going on."

Mr. Marron told me, "If you have any difficulties, go to Valley Medical Center. Ask the ER physicians to call me."

"Mr. Marron, I would not take our dog to Valley Medical Center."

Then, Mr. Marron joyfully said, "You're going to be okay; you're not hurt. You are a VIP, a very important person."

Mr. Marron told me to go home and wait. I was perplexed needless to say.

"This is going to be a big Christmas. People are coming from Connecticut to visit you," he said.

I replied, "My father, Colonel Lindbergh, is he here? I know this, he is either here or on his way, and my siblings, are they coming?"

Moose Marron gave me approving chuckles. "All I can tell you is that you're a VIP, and you have a big surprise."

I heard this a great deal, a big surprise that never seemed to come and filled with empty promises.

KEVIN HUSTED, SR.

1969 to 1990 - The Awesome Sequels

The schemed illegal drug blast to my brain kept me stunned for many months. My obsession to search for my parents and siblings intensified, kept me motivated. I would liken the drug blast to my brain to a mountain climber working the mountain to reach for the top with broken bones. The killing scene of Ms. Adele Welsh relived in my psyche. Cryptomnesia blooms reverberated in my psyche, and the reality of the damage sent me into research to rework my brain mass.

I called FBI Agent Malcolm B. "Buck" Sample. He directed me to a neurologist who conducted an electroencephalograph that evidenced intense brain activity. When the drug blast roared and red, blue flame flashed out, my brain popped for days, which I likened to the cracking of crackle, bubble gum. For weeks a silhouette of the scales of justice was always in view.

Many FBI agents were in on the exhausting investigation and head game activity, inclusive of sheriff deputies, police officers, and deputy district attorneys. FBI records and witnesses will evidence the schemed convert activities and all the players.

One early evening, an FBI agent showed me the Spectra physics high percentile analysis that was completed on me.

I stared at him. "Sir, does it look like I am Lindbergh?"

He told me, "It looks like you could be. I am en route to Los Angeles. When I return, I will call you."

The FBI agent never called.

On entering the Hyatt House lobby, I walked over to greet FBI Agent "Charles A." Malcolm B. "Buck" Sample. Buck stood to attention and introduced me to FBI Agent Sanborn who said, "Buck tells me you're a VIP."

"Where are my parents? I have checked the Hyatt registry; they're not here. Are they in Hillsborough?"

Buck again told me, "You're a VIP; you have a big surprise coming!"

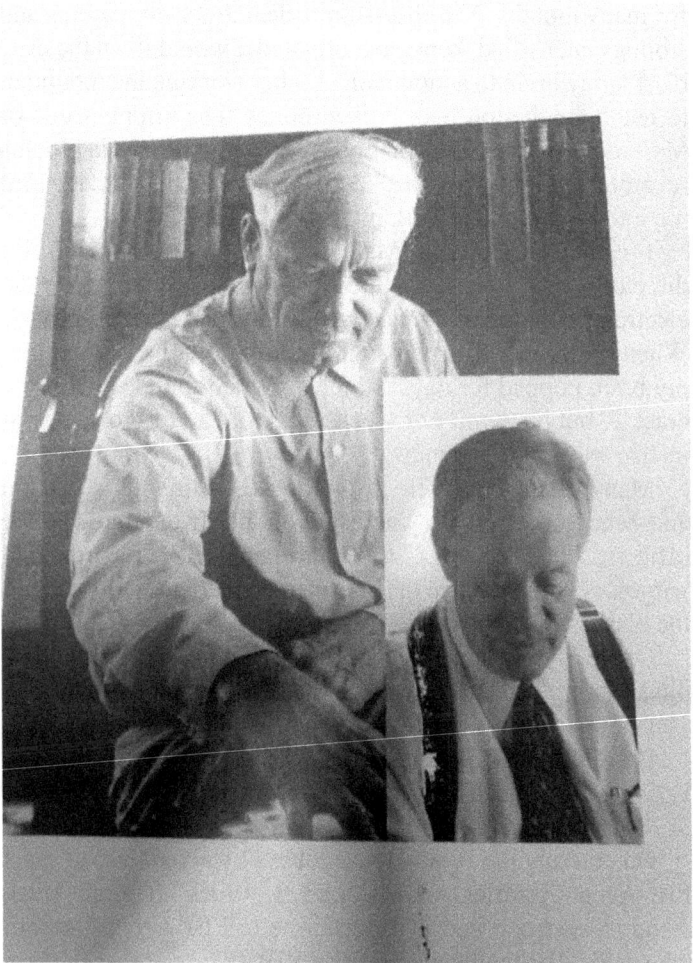

Charles A. Lindbergh, Sr. on the left. A picture he carried of Charles A. Lindbergh, Sr. on the right.

KEVIN HUSTED, SR.

Kay had filed for divorce. The Husteds and certain Italian figures had influenced her against me.

My son Kevin and I moved from our comfortable residence. Out of mercy for Kay, I gave her the residence at 1395 Sierra Avenue, San Jose, California.

To keep our sons well occupied, at 2:30 p.m. daily, I drove them from St. Leo School to the Pruneridge Golf Course. Brad and Kevin went through golf school twice and drove golf balls daily.

FBI agents and local authorities took an observation. I saw my father, Colonel Lindbergh, surrounded by local authorities. My father and authorities were some distance to my left and forward. This occurred when I was approached by Win. W. Baltz. My sons were driving golf balls when Mr. Baltz gave me his business card. Mr. Baltz invited me to call him and to bring my son Kevin to stay with his wife and him at their residence in Darien, Connecticut.

"Things will work out," Mr. Baltz told me. The appearance of Mr. Baltz was like my father.

Several days passed. I was in the Hyatt House lobby when Leslie Baltz, warmly and kindly approached me saying to me, "You look like a Lindbergh. It's been so long ago. We need more evidence."

Miss Baltz invited me to breakfast the next morning. When I showed at her Sunnyvale, CA apartment, she was gone. Ms. Baltz was with United Airlines.

I searched the Hyatt lobby one evening when physicist LA "Lee" Hurt, who was dining with a very attractive well-dressed blonde, motioned me to visit. I sat across from the woman, and Lee Hurt. When Lee failed to introduce me to Anne, I stood and introduced myself. We shook hands; she would not give her name.

"Lee, is this beautiful lady, my sister Anne Lindbergh?"

I replied, "Lee, an FBI agent tells me the spectraphysics test is a close match; tell me I'm a Lindbergh."

Lee said, "Could be; time will tell."

With tears in my eyes, I told Anne, "I love you. I believe you're my sister," and then dismissed myself.

Another Lindbergh

I finished a glass of buttermilk. The time was evening.

In the back of me was a row booth. Mike Jack and several FBI agents were seated with what I believe was my brother Land M. Lindbergh. As I exited, I stopped to greet Mike Jack and the young man in blue jacket and white trousers who followed me to the coffee shop entrance.

He then said, "You best keep your mouth shut about this investigation, and you're being Lindbergh, or you're going to be shot dead with a police pistol."

I was shaken.

Alphonse Capone

At the law office of Thomas Salciccia, I was shown the Palm Island residence of Alphonse Capone and an interior room. The dining room furnishings vigorously evoked in me a strong memory of once being there.

The cryptomnesia memory blooms vigorously appeared.

June 22, 1970

Jerome Gatto and his fiancée gave me a birthday party at Original Joe's Restaurant, San Jose, California. Jerome said to me, "Your birth date is June 22, 1930, not November 18, 1930; in the future, you will understand."

KEVIN HUSTED, SR.

Roland Orwig gave assistance to the FBI investigation and surveillance. In the Hyatt House, Mr. Orwig contracted me to his Sunset Life Insurance General Agency, no question asked. I did not do well. I earned a gold watch and one week at The Camelback Inn.

Mr. Orwig then gave me a policy card on Ed Osborn and told me I must see Ed Osborn that day. "I have an appointment set up. You are to assess all of Ed's policies."

I met with Ed Osborn at his Vista Del Lago townhouse.

Mr. Osborn seated me across from him at his large dining table and asked me to audit his many policies. My intuition sensed a scheme going down.

In front of Mr. Osborn was a large picture album and ends of pictures sticking out under the album. Mr. Osborn went to the bathroom. I stood, lifted the album, and shuffled through the pictures of me prior to my kidnap and pictures of my parents and my youth. When Osborn returned, I was at work doing a ledger of his policies. Soon the big surprise arrived.

FBI Agent Ken Sheets had arrived and kindly explained, "If you don't mind; I need to visit with Ed."

FBI Agent Ken Sheets stood and leaned to the right of Ed removing small pictures from an envelope. The two shuffled pictures and murmured agreements as they observed my pictures and my face and ears.

In a short time, the frame of days Mr. Orwig booked me into three other policy service interviews with Osborn. In each interview, FBI Agent Ken Sheets arrived and worked with Ed on their observations.

I REMEMBER

1993

I located Ed Osborn in San Rafael, CA. By telephone, I inquired about the observation activity with FBI Agent Ken Sheets. He was alarmed that I knew what was going on.

Ed Osborn then said, "I cannot talk to you. Don't call back."

A short time later, Ed Osborn died of cancer. Ed Osborn was a friend of my father, Colonel Lindbergh. Ed was a commercial pilot who had flown for Frank Sinatra, Attorney Jim Boccardo, actors Danny Kaye and Gene Autry, and the Gallo Winery Company.

1968 to 1970 – Federal Bureau of Investigation – 1770 East Hamilton Avenue, Second Floor, San Jose, CA.

I visited the FBI office. On arriving, I found FBI agents on the stairway at all open ground entrances and the Director of the FBI. J. Edgar Hoover, on the second-floor walkway flanked by FBI agents. At last, I would meet face to face the Chief, who I was so often told by Myrtle Husted to go see should I have trouble. On the staircase, an attorney gave me his business card, asking that I call him, "You will need my services."

He was from Fresno, CA.

I was not allowed to visit FBI Agent "Charles A" Malcolm B. "Buck" Sample that day.

1971

Roland Orwig invited me to a meeting that involved Matson Shipping Lines. There were many young people; pictures were flashed. Orwig was a master at working head games. He once got angry toward me telling me that drug blast could not have hurt me.

In the time frame 1971 through the retirement, "Charles A" Malcolm B. 'Buck' Sample attempted to drive me insane, assisted by FBI Agent Adrian D. Coulter, FBI Agent Phil Crumb, Sgt. Stan Shaver and FBI Agent Jim Page. When I would call to visit FBI Agent Buck Sample, he would, on many calls, use a sound device that would send a vibration of low sound and high decibel. The results were brain shattering, like a concussion.

FBI Agent Sample circulated rumors that I was gay, a homosexual. Homosexuals harassed me.

In 1969 to the 1970-timeframe, I received a policy service card. The appointment was a homosexual; and supposed relative of District Attorney Louis Bergna.

FBI Agent Coulter took over when FBI Agent Buck Sample retired.

1985 - FBI Agent Coulter

FBI Agent Coulter and I entered the rear door of the Prune Yard One Towers building. FBI Agent Coulter turned back to me saying, "Now you know your real name."

I replied, "Lindbergh."

On another occasion in the Tower One Bar, FBI Agent Coulter told me Buck Sample was in Germany. "He has all your money."

On another occasion, I met by coincidence Mrs. Coulter at National Semiconductor, or it was arranged? She looked identical to the frumpy blond cashier setting up her register in the coffee shop the morning I was drugged. She appeared very nervous.

I REMEMBER

Vladimir "Vlado" Kovalik, Physicist, Nuclear Physicist, Oceanography Science, Computer Science, and Scientist for a Russian Space Scientist

Vlado has told me the cosmonauts are excited at my being alive and would like to meet me. On September 9, 1999, he told me he bought a Belera, an Italian 700-year-old apartment building sixty kilometers north of Rome, Italy. This fits his image as he relates as an international playboy.

Since 1951, Vlado and my brother, Jon Lindbergh, have traveled the world, and rafted the toughest rivers, climbed Shasta, developed innovations for underwater research, and shared many other adventures worldwide. Vlado has told me this about my brother Jon M. Lindbergh, "Avoid communicating with him because Jon thinks I have tried to help you."

Vlado said he had asked Jon for hair samples to do a DNA test, but Jon became angry at the requests and told Vlado, "I never want to see or talk to Charles again."

Jon angrily declined to join me in DNA analysis. He refused to accept mail from my attorney or me. He has changed his phone to unlisted.

In 1960, Vladimir directed me to Martin Litton, who he had been friends with for more than forty years. Litton said, "Charles, when the time is right, we will meet; I will share with you what I know. You are going to have to water down your story, or you will hurt Jon."

When visiting the Bay Area, Vladimir resides at the home of Bob and Founce Rand. Attorney Rand knows the inside scoop on Kovalik's communication with Jon M. Lindbergh pertaining to my being the kidnapped Lindbergh's son.

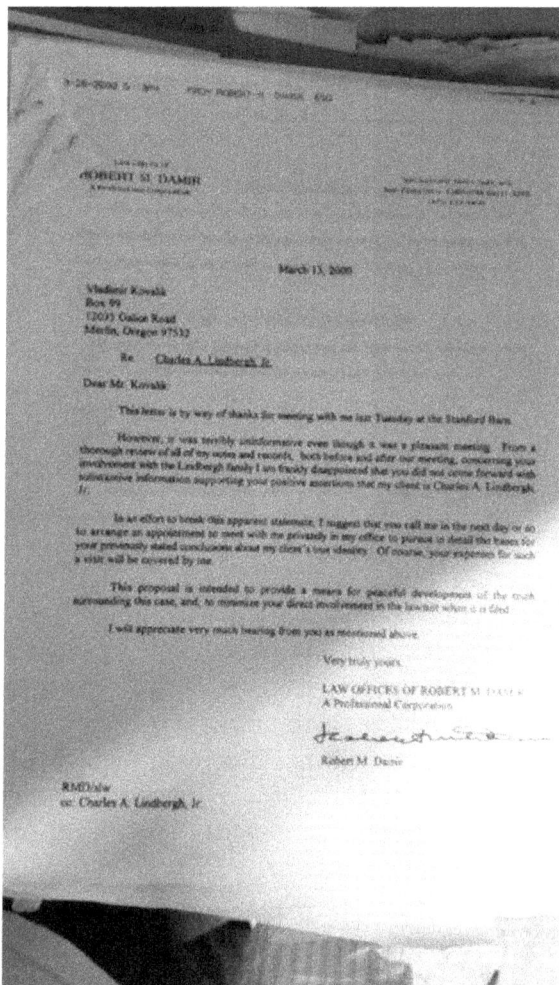

Attorney representing Charles A. Lindbergh, Jr., tried on countless occasions for people to step forward with the truth.

I REMEMBER

1972 - Thanksgiving Day Dinner

My son, Kevin, and I were guests of Carolyn Faith Myers.

From 1971 to 1972, my son Kevin and I attended the San Jose Baptist Church with Reverend Clarence Sands. Unknown to me, FBI special agents, sheriff's deputies, San Jose, California police officers, and deputy district attorneys also attended the church.

Carolyn Myers, a career Pacific Bell employee in the Special Services Division, at that time, was an attractive woman with two children, a boy, and a girl close in age to my son, Kevin.

Carolyn invited us to Thanksgiving breakfast and dinner. When we arrived, she told me, "You have a big surprise – a surprise visitor you have not seen since 1969."

At this time, I looked good on the outside, but internally I was hanging on to my mental faculties like a gold miner clutching a large gold nugget; the result of the illegal drug blast to my brain.

It was noontime when the surprise guest arrived. The guest was L.A. "Lee" Hurt, the physicist who performed the high percentile match Spectra-Physics test for the FBI. Lee Hurt was a non-descript, scientist type – a curmudgeon, subtle, calm patient, dry sense of humor, master of head games. Lee Hurt was seated.

I said in a calm manner, "Lee, I'll sit across from you and one over so you can't drug my mind. If my memory serves me, you are a friend of the FBI Agent Buck Sample."

Lee Hurt pulled a grin and murmured, "Yum, yum, yum; allow me to teach you how to taste for chemicals in your coffee."

I replied, "Lee, Buck Sample plotted and carried out the illegal drug blast to my brain."

He then stated, "You're not hurt, no brain damage is done; you'll be okay."

I said, "Lee, a day will come when I will take Buck Sample to Court."

He replied, "Hogwash; it will never happen."

Lee Hurt told me there were many people involved. He then asked me if I knew Adrian Coulter.

"No," I said.

He then told me that Agent Bumpers was an FBI agent, adding, "Buck Sample has all the answers you're looking for. Go talk to Buck."

At that point, I inquired, "Lee, the evening in the Hyatt House Coffee Shop, you invited me to your table. Was the beautiful blond lady with you, my sister Anne? You would not tell me her name; she just smiled."

I waited for a response before I asked, "Is this my sister, Anne Lindbergh? When I asked, you replied, 'Time will tell.' I then said, Lee, tell me now, was that my sister, Anne?"

He stated, "It could be; you could be Lindbergh; time will tell."

Next, he asked me, "Do you know Vladimir Kovalik? He is a physicist."

I replied, "No."

Lee stated, "He knows you. Do you know Robert Shattuck?"

"No," I said.

He proceeded to tell me that I should get to know them both and added, "Bob is a pilot. When Bob returns to the area, I will introduce you. Bob is a friend of Vladimir Kovalik, and they are friends of your siblings... Oops! I had better not say that or I'll get into trouble. You ask too many questions, and I talk too much. Go talk to Buck."

Lee Hurt then gave me his business card and invited me to visit him at his Spectra-Physics lab. I called him afterward on the phone to visit, but he declined to answer my questions.

1976 - LA "Lee" Hurt introduced me to Robert M. "Bob" Shattuck, Pilot

"Bob" Shattuck was a somewhat nondescript individual. In 1980 he married Viola, Shoemaker, aka Bi, a longtime friend of Reverend Marvin G. Rickard, pastor of Los Gatos Christian Church.

Cocky, arrogant, and discreetly bigoted, in 1976 Bob Shattuck informed me that I would never be able to trace his connections. He then stated, "I could be with the FBI, the CIA, the KGB. I know Agent Buck Sample. I know all about you. When I leave you and Kevin, you will not be able to trace me. I am here to put you in top shape so I can unite you with your family, Colonel and Anne Lindbergh and your siblings. Your brothers are Jon, Land, and Scott, and your sisters are Anne and Reeve. They are all friends of mine. Jon and I have a mutual friend, Vladimir Kovalik. Vlado has KGB connections; it isn't likely you will meet with Vladimir."

KEVIN HUSTED, SR.

1976 - 1980

I would liken Bob Shattuck to a shadow. He would often be gone two, three weeks at a time. When in the area, however, Bob was at our residence daily, and on occasion, flew Kevin and me to airshows and fly-in breakfasts.

I perceived that Bob played consecutive head games. He would demand that I recall memories of life before my kidnapping. At any moment, Bob might stop and say, "I must call Kovalik, or call Vlado or Vladimir, or Jon, or Reeve, or Land or Anne."

Most calls were to Vlado.

Bob would go absolutely nuts when I demanded that he introduce me to Vladimir.

When I would ask, "What does Vladimir look like," he would say, "You will never know. It's not for you to know. In nineteen sixty-nine and nineteen seventy, Vlado and I observed you."

Robert M. "Bob" Shattuck contracted with a famous artist by the name Kiester for Kevin, and I have to obtain a three-feet by four-foot painting of my father, Colonel C.A. Lindbergh, and the *Spirit of St. Louis*. I sent a color photograph to General Jimmy Doolittle.

At 9:00 p.m., General Doolittle called me, directing me to display the painting in the Fairmount Hotel Lobby, in San Francisco, California. He also stated that I should take the painting to Arthur Anderson, a Certified Public Accountancy firm. He said, "They are expecting you, and they will place the painting in the Fairmount Hotel."

The General then informed me, "You are my guest."

The General and I visited about forty–five minutes at the beginning of the closed-door Lindbergh Memorial Luncheon.

Bob Shattuck then told me, "You are going to meet your brother, Jon. Let me do the talking. Jon has a pretty bad temper."

We met; I stood, Jon sat, and Bob sat by the twin marble columns inside the corner entrance. Jon would not shake hands. He looked me over, dropped his head, shook his head, looked at Bob, then got up slowly, and walked away. Somewhere there are many photographs of this luncheon.

1977 – 1980

Bob Shattuck called one Saturday night, and said, "You and Kevin be ready early tomorrow morning (Sunday). I'm flying you to the Columbia Fly-in Breakfast. Jon and Land might be there."

We flew in a new Beach Bonanza owned by United Airlines pilot Johnny Wheel. We were seated for breakfast in the Columbia hangar. At some distance away, Bob visited with who could have been Land Lindbergh and family. The family looked toward Kevin and me and laughed. Bob returned to us. We toured Columbia, CA; from a payphone, Bob called Vladimir.

In the same 1977 - 1980-time frame, Bob Shattuck called on another Saturday night and said, "You and Kevin be ready early in the morning."

We took off in a six-passenger Cherokee flying southwest over the Pacific Ocean. Bob then informed me Jon or Land were supposed to pick up a family in Watsonville, CA. We circled a hangar, and in the shade of the hangar door, I could see an elegantly attired woman, a well-dressed, very young lady, and a well-dressed small boy. We taxied to an estimated distance of seventy feet from the hangar. The temperature was over one hundred degrees.

Bob spoke rudely and demanded we remain in the plane. "Do not visit us," he warned.

In the shade of the plane, Kevin and I observed Bob visiting with the woman and small boy. I searched for the woman's face. Could this be my mother, Anne? Shortly after, we were again in flight, and I asked Bob if that was my mother, Anne.

"It's not your business who it is. Shut up."

We landed at Reid Hillview airport in San Jose. Bob called Vladimir.

1976 – 1980

Kevin and I attended many air shows as guests of Bob Shattuck. During this period of engagements to Vi Shoemaker, Bob became quite arrogant making directed comments such as, "You're not showing any progress. I've been told to cut you off."

At this time, Kevin and I were attending the Los Gatos Christian Church. We then became rudely snubbed by Vi Shoemaker, Bob Shattuck, and Rev. Marvin G. Rickard.

God, however, I believe has His own timing, One Sunday, Kevin, and I were in the auditorium annex. Kevin pointed, and said, "Dad, there's Bob Shattuck."

In the auditorium, about eight seats away were Bob and someone who looked like a Lindbergh. I sensed I was being watched. I turned around toward the annex door entrance and observed a well-dressed man with a grin, in appearance similar to myself. He walked out and just then Bob Shattuck and the individual who resembled a Lindbergh stood up. This person then thrust his arm, finger pointed to me and dramatically yelled, "If he goes to church here, I will not ever come here again."

Kevin and I quietly walked out.

1980

During this time, Bob Shattuck informed me that Jon had directed him to draw up a release of the painting. "You're going to sign the release."

Through Bob, I am told, "You cannot have the painting of your father. We are cutting you off. You're showing no signs of progress."

Bob drove me to Scribe Secretarial Services. The owner is a friend to Bill Nelson, a friend of Jon's. Janet Brooner typed the release at no charge.

We delivered the signed release to the Nakashima and Boynton Law Firm.

Through 1986 Bob Shattuck visited Kevin on occasion at Hadley's Market in Vallco Shopping Center, Cupertino, CA. Kevin was the Manager. He had taken the store from a loss to a profit.

KEVIN HUSTED, SR.

1980 Bob Shattuck told me about Bob Chamberlin, Ph.D., and his success in drawing up identities (ref. 1980 results).

1992 to 1995

Susan Adams, with Scribe Secretarial Services, accomplished all my business and word processing work. Unknown to Susan Adams or Janet Brooner, I was doing business with them to learn about their connection to my brother, Jon M. Lindbergh.

It was in 1976 Robert M. "Bob" Shattuck informed me of their being friends with Jon and Bill Nelson.

Bob had Janet Brooner type a release pointing to the painting of my father, Colonel C.A. Lindbergh, which my brother, Jon, had demanded to Bob that I immediately sign.

In this time frame, Janet and Susan made frequent sly innuendoes. On one occasion, Ms. Jan Daukins began visiting the office. Well-dressed and speaking a few words, Ms. Daukins often sat back of Ms. Adams on the official guest bench. Ms. Daukins told me she had just received a writing desk. She then asked if I would visit her apartment to assemble the desk.

I kindly declined.

"I bet my mother would like to meet you," she said. "She lives back East."

I asked, "Connecticut?"

She said nothing in reply.

On occasion, Ms. Daukins would stand to my left as I worked with Ms. Adams on my word processing. Once,

Ms. Adams turned and said humorously, "Let me see your fingernails. Look, they're clean!"

I wondered what the problem as Ms. Daukins was eyeing my outstretched hands.

Another time when I was standing patiently and calmly by Ms. Adams, I stepped back to view the mysterious Ms. Daukins and wanted to ask her if she could be my sister Anne Lindbergh.

Ms. Daukins looked at me and said, "Are you doing this for money?"

I replied sharply, saying, "Money and justice, and I intend to visit my mother!"

Ms. Daukins' hair was unusually long like a fall. Ms. Daukins then told me she has an ankle birth defect and asked me what she should do.

I said, "I can find you the finest physician in Napa Valley, California."

On another occasion, I visited Bill Nelson and his wife, and we dined together. Bill Nelson brought up the 1969 to 1970 FBI investigation and said, "Your father would have suffered embarrassment had he accepted you."

Joseph Cerrito, he indicated, was involved. "The Colonel and the FBI closed down your being identified," he said. "Charles, you should make friends with Attorney Robert Bryan, attorney for the Hauptmann family. I'm sure he has information to help you write your story. You look like the Colonel."

Of course, I listened.

Bill told me. "Jon is not happy with your story."

That was my last visit with Bill Nelson or with his wife. We have had conversations over the phone to discuss locating my brother, Jon.

In 1995, I called Ms. Daukins, but the number was disconnected. A DMV search produced zero information.

In 1998 I asked Vladimir, "Do you know Jan Dawkins?"

Vlado chuckled and said, "I've heard the name."

"Vlado," I asked, "Could it be Anne?"

Vlado replied, "Anne is sharp and cunning."

1994 - Responses by Telephone Made by Vladimir Kovalik and I During Phone Communications

- "My God, Charles, you sound just like Jon and the old man. I have a lot of information on you going way back."

- "No, I didn't know you were at John Deere. Please tell me about your job at John Deere Planter Works."

- "I can't wait to shake your hand. I admire your courage."

- "Charles, I am going to do everything possible to unite you with your siblings. Mom should know you're still alive; Anne would live longer. You need to meet with your mother."

- "What has been done to you should never have happened. It's a shame, and I will do all that I can help you."

- "I'm going to call Jon right now and ask him to do a DNA."

- "I know for certain you are Charles A. Lindbergh, Jr. Your siblings know you're their brother."

- "Charles, I visited Jon at his home in North Bend, Washington. I asked for hair samples to do a DNA, but Jon wouldn't give me a hair sample. Jon tells he doesn't want to ever see you or talk to you."

- "Hang in, Charles; don't give up. You will come out okay, you'll see."

- "I am acquainted with Buck Sample. That was a long time ago. God, you got a memory."

- "Der Spiegel, Focus – I have spent time with the top editors of these magazines, showing them your files. We need DNA. They tell me if you are a Lindbergh, we will make him a millionaire overnight. We will come to America and fly his family to Germany. You will be given a castle."

- "German television is exciting! We need DNA."

- "All of them believe the polygraph. We are in need of the DNA sample."

- "The CEO of Mercedes Benz is my friend. I have talked to him about your doing commercials. We need the DNA."

1996 - Stanford Barn, California Café, Stanford, California

Adua, my fourth wife, and I arrived early so we could view the arrival. We are well inside the Café entrance. I pointed out, "Adua, there is Vladimir on the right. I do not know the other men."

She replied, "Charles, how do you know that's Vlado?"

"I recognize him from the nineteen sixty-nine and seventy FBI investigations in the Hyatt House."

"My God, what a memory you have. I should take memory lessons from you."

We then met Attorney Bob Rand and the bearded Martin Litton. We sat in the Café rear patio. Around the table to my left was my wife, Adua, and Martin Litton was on my right. Bob Rand was to the right of Martin Litton and Vladimir to the left of my wife with Vladimir directly across from me.

From the beginning of our visit to the close, Vladimir repeatedly expressed to me and everyone around the table, "My God, Charles, you look like the old man; the Colonel. You have the same genetic physical animation, you sit like Jon, and you sound like Jon. This is like old times visiting with Jon. I am convinced you are the

Lindbergh boy." Vlado then asked, "What does your son in Montana think of this?"

I replied, "We haven't communicated in years. Vlado, tell me why my father rejected me during the nineteen sixty-nine and seventies investigation."

Vlado explained, "The old man was a teetotaler, and was not pleased with your drinking wine. He was also not happy and would have been humiliated because he had lied in the Hauptmann trial."

When we were ordering lunch, Vlado asked, "Do you still drink?"

KEVIN HUSTED, SR.

MY CASE AGAINST DON W. HUSTED, SR.

I can't end my book without sharing with you the pain and turmoil I encountered at the hands of Don W. Husted, Sr. I wrote him a letter explaining the details and my feelings on January 25, 1985. In a way, I was venting.

Editor's Note

Instead of transcribing the eight-page letter, which is a repeat of some information contained in this book, I felt it was best for you to see and read what Charles A. Lindbergh, Jr., wrote and let you decide for yourself his turmoil and pain that existed in his life. The next couple of pages are from his typewritten notes he kept for his autobiography.

I REMEMBER

Rev. Don W. Husted, Sr.

In the summer of 1976 at your request we met on the parking lot
of the Factory Shopping Center in Campbell, California; you
ask my foregiveness but refused to discuss what I was foregiving
you for. On December 12, 1983 I rec'd a letter frosted with
Bible screptures, you inquired if I had consulted with Marvin
Richard (minister of Los Gatos Christian Church) on restoring
a relationship with you. I never considered such a move, we
never had a relationship and never will. I have endured fifty
years of your viciousness, crimes, abuse and being humiliated.
You have gone uncontested uhtill now. For years you have
functioned behind the shield of Christianity, your fury, viciousness
corruption covered by your ability to skillfully lie and
manipulate people to carry out your dirty work. What you were
not aware of is Agents of the Federal Bureau of Investigation
frequently kept a surveilance on me as far back a 1936. In
recent years F.B.I. agents developed reflection studies. I
am not your son. I was born June 22, 1930. I can endure positive
testing of the following account by Federal Authorities applying
polygraph, voiceprint tests and applied Hypnosis. Some data
is all ready recorded in Medical files and F.B.I. files.

Chronological Account:

1935, June - Arrid summer: Location 241 So. Volustia Str.,
Wichita, KS. (residence of your parents Loren McFadden and
Myrtle Husted.) we are in the north front bedroom. Crime: you
are sexually molesting me; frequency of your abuse is unknown.

1935 through 1943 - 55% to 65% my time was spent residing with
your parents at 241 So. Volustia Str. Up to 1939 when your
parents moved into their new home in the Klassen District at
2101 So. Oliver Str., Wichita, Kansas; your physical violence
on me often neccessitated relatives physically restraining you.
I was often beat black, blood running from my eyes, nose, mouth,
ears, there is evidence of early bone damage to my back. When
residing with you, Viola in the Kansas City, Kansas, Missouri
area my grade level at Francis Willard School dropped to D-F-.
We resided at 331 No. 30th Street, Kansas City, Kan. Here
I was beat, locked in the bedroom closet, left to hunger, threatened
to be drowned in the Arkansas River. I would fall asleep at
my classroom desk. I suffered a form of Dysflexia. Oft times
I laid awake throughout the night as you and Viola battled with
your selfish emotions, oft times I sat the night on your suit-
caste hanging on to your hand, jacket, and Viola weeping tears,
pleading for peace. In your fury I have hugged the floor board
of your auto as you drove at speeds up to 115 MPH through city
streets or to race the El Capiton to a crossing. You were an
ambulance chaser. I've visited with you many a late night
crash viewing decapitated people, I recall walking the railroad

tracks through pieces of human flesh, parts of bodies. On Sunday nights you, Rev. Vince Parker, his sweetheart Betty partied at a Coney Island Restaurant in the Red light District of Kansas City, Missouri - here I slept in your car, roamed up, down the street. My favorite place was a Black Night Club Titled The Golden Jubilee, a brass band played, beautifull black women danced. I was lifted from the open doorway to the bar where I was entertained with coke and 7 up. At home with you parents my grade level at Hillside County School would rise to A-A+. My life was at peace here, a self contained lad I was busy building model planes, box kites, sketching early American planes, three stage rockets, learning to work a wood lathe. Here we had calm daily devotions. Here I was taught to trust in Lord Jesus Christ first, J. Edgar Hoover, Chief of the F.B.I. second.

My success patterns were consistant. The horrible hopelessness experienced when residing with you was not to be noticed. The country school managed by Audrey Houston was unique. My home work; my projects were quality. Then came shock and trauma. March 1941, I'm in shock, horrible nightmares, fill my sleepless nights. My book covers, binders I covered with these symbols, to close my eyes ment. seeing a lady hanging upside down her body ripped and bleeding, neck sliced open, nipples cut off. This trauma healed after some six weeks. The crime I saw sunk below the surface of my concious mind into the subconcious. Only to surface years later.

Shortly after the slaying of Adele Welsh, you overdosed on Aspirin, at four a.m. Women from the church came to heat plates in hot towels applying to your back and chest, as they poured hot milk down your stomach. You clung to the iron bed rails, twisting them. As you relaxed, the church ladies left the room, you motioned for Mrs. Peperdine to listen, she bent over. I was in the doorway, she turned from you, here face grief stricken and ushered me into bed.

In September 1984, I by telephone charged you will slaying Adele Welsh, you cringed, as you cringed you said I quote: I will break your neck. It was you who murdered Adele Welsh in March 1941. The night of the murder you had with you a long U.S. Army wool trench coat. You left me asleep in your auto, I got out, walked into the house where I saw the slaying through a crack in the door. This accounts for the shock and trauma I experienced. It was I who found in the rear of your dirt floor garage (331 No. 30th Str., K.C., KA) a bloody gunney sack and instrument. You took the instrument, placed it in a cigar box and buried it down stream under water, under an overhanging pear tree. (After undergoing an intense investigation in 1968, the County Squire (Kansas City, Missouri) published a uniqe editorial on the slaying of Adele Welsh, which I acquired from then Chief Police, Joe Kelly, who later became Chief of the F.B.I.

I REMEMBER

(1955 at John Deere Planter works I was advised by Ret. Lt. Col. Guy W. Ade, that you were a suspect in the Adele Welsh slaying and the Black Dahlia slaying in 1943. AT the time I was aware of his source. I was also advised to my identity. The Lt. Col. pleaded with me along with others not to enter business with you in May 1956. They had secured information you would attempt to or do me in. I was advised not to sign business agreements with you or make you beneficiary on a Life Insurance policy. These fine friends of mine were accurate. Motivated by your letter where you claimed to be dieing you hadn't long to live, you claimed a desire to justify your injustice to me. I was nieve, still a slave to your years of battery. (see chronological report and my autobiography about to be completed).

(1942-43) Residing with your parents at 2101 So. Oliver Str., Wichita, KS at the time I was eleven going on twelve, working a summer job at Ruby's Rexall Drug, seven days per week at 11.00 per week. Then you came from California to pick me up, (you and Helen) I trembled at the thought of going with you two I had a good job occassionally caddied at the Meadow Lake *Lark* Golf Course. I recall well how, Vince Parker, your friends nicknamed you Doc. Doc for what, you were not a doctor, your house calls I often traveled with you to the wee hours of the morning observing people die. We arrived in Los Angeles, CA at the Commadore Apartments just off Wilshire Blvd. After the connections you made at Biola, which impressed me as a lad, I could not understand your abuse to me, your wife, Helen was vicious. Then came the Black Dahlia slaying, News media and Homicide was looking for a character in a 1941 Black Mercury and the name "Doc". You made it clear that the name "Doc" was never to be used again, we were moving to San Luis Obispo, CA. We moved into 1118 Buschon Str., a stucco house owned by Clarence Ferrar. From this location you set up your church, Real Estate and Insurance office. One of your first church deacons was George Miller & his wife Madge residing with them was Annie a beautiful Mexican girl. You and Helen brought her to live with us. Often times Annie was lethargic, drunk on wine (red). You, Helen took Annie frequently into the bedroom, locked the doors, I observed the sexual abuse on Anne, till you patched over the key holes.

Then one night late I came home to find Annie, excessively drunk, nude on the kitchen floor. She attempted suicide. I called in Mrs. Babb. You and Helen were away. When you returned you were violently angry that I called in Mrs. Babb.

In San Luis Obispo, CA, my first job was a paper boy, boxing, delviery 250 papers daily @ 44.00/mo. Inc. I then went to work for Austins Confection and Restaurant. Then moved by Chas Simon and Steve Zeagan, a personal friend of Randolp Hearst. On Saturday mornings I washed all the downtown store windows on Higuera and Monteray. Three years at Austins won me friends and fame. I then mvoedyon to being stock boy for Montgomery Ward, then to Purina Feed. With exception of my window washing money, you confiscated all my earnings from, the paper route,

KEVIN HUSTED, SR.

Austins

Autins, Montgomery Ward, you kept the cash. (see autobiograph
for all details) Then I got a summer job with Faulstch Bro.
Brick Co. at 2.75/hr. The townspeople had little respect for
you. One grave mistake you made was beating me black, it was
a rainey day, a Sunday afternoon. I was beat black, I called
Superior Court Judge Ray Lyon. He drove down to his chambers,
I slipped away to meet him at the jail entrance. In his chambers,
Judge Lyon had me stripped to my shorts. The judge was levid.
He set you straight. The beatings did not stop. Then as President
of the Real Estate Board, you blacklisted Charles Asbaugh,
cost him his license, claiming he had stole $3000 cash from your
office. My theory is you stole the cash. You, Helen then moved
to the Fair Oaks District of Arrayo Grande, CA, you had acquired
the ranch house from Mrs. Walt Waterman. My autobiography
illustrates the rough time I had in school. How you insisted
I shave under my arms, a characteristic of a homosexual. My
classmates scoffed me. Never in my life have I been gay.
You bastard.

I outlived that shame. What no one realized because I was
capable of doing a good days work was my Psyche had been bruised
and healed so often that hopelessness shorted out my ableness
to pursue a higher education.

Your bastardization created a condition that cost me a Harvard
University Education, a career in the Federal Bureau of Investigation,
a successful stint with the U.S. Navy. What a loss; the condition
cost my fine sons, my x-wife, Kay a good life. Ten thousand
480 hours later in 1983, I succeeded in making a full recovery
applying a unique thinking process, vitamins, and rigerous
exercise.

I now have a new wife, she is precious, tender she deserves
the finest; I recall vividly how your friend Sasha Woolery
attempted to malign me to my wife in 1984.
The days of you, your family attempting to stop our progress
is over. She is a talented lady, a muscian and history buff.

Little did you know that while employed at Austin, Mr. Simon,
Mr. Cochran entertained me at Cochrans Coffee Shop with F.B.I.
agents, I sipped down a pineapple milkshake.
my father Colonel Lindbergh   *an*
Then came a gross mistake on your part. Your wife Helen put
the make on me. It was June, 1951, I pushed her away she fell
over a planter, I picked her up. As she shook her fist in
my face, you will pay for this. I did when you arrived home,
she ushered you to the back bedroom. I was a courageous kid,
with a keen sense of justice. I'm still that way. You came
down the hall, no explanation was I allowed. You beat me till
blood ran from my nose, ears, eyes, mouth. You kicked me up
against the walls, into the fire place and physically threw
me around the room. I crawled to my room, climbed up into
my closet and loaded my 22 cal. carbine rifle. turned to
go blow you away, when a still small voice said, no, let him

-4-

EXHIBIT F

189

be, kill him will ruin your life, your opportunity to join the
F.B.I. I got out an old Navy foot locker, given me by Walt
Waterman, packed all my valuables into it nailed it shut, and
walked down the Hwy for the greyhound bus Dept. with a Indian
Head nickle in my pocket. A call to your parents confirmed
a ticket for Wichita, Kansas. Three days, three nights I traveled,
eating a Babe Ruth candy bar.

Arriving in Wichita, Kansas, back into the residence of your
parents I found myself healing. I also found myself in need
of liquor, attending El Dorado Junior College, playing right
end, I often found myself drunk. I had succeeded in transfering
all Navy Bupers from the 12th Naval District to Olathe NAS.
Beat hopeless I could never make flight school. We didn't
know what it was that kept me from going the extra mile; it
was for certain I was a winner at what ever I applied myself
to. I could get a Navy SNJ off the ground, but never get it
down. The FBI was still my goal, Harvard University was ever
on my mind but I couldn't pursue the course. My self worth
was down. I looked good. Inside I didn't feel good.

My God little did I realize at John Deere that my friend were
right. Entering the Insurance Business with you in May 1956
proved them right. I earned a B+ average on the correspondence
course with Golden Gate College of Insurance half the lessons
(we discovered) were never turned in through your agency.
I was an A av. student with Alexander Hamilton Bus. Institute
A div. of Fordham University, New York, New York. Prior to
joining your agency, I had done a Market Research at the University
of Iowa on San Luis Obispo County. In your agency I soon discovered your gratuities, promises were never kept. You charged
me with stealing $2300 from the office kitty. I never went
through your files or drawers untill Mr. Evans, who you had
bought out his agency came to me one evening asking if I would
check your books that something was wrong with your paying
off the agency accounts. A check showed you were transfering
a percentage to other companies.

(Let us travel back to 1943 or 1944 when you drove with me
along to Cambrian Pines, California, you stopped front of the
Bank of America, you robbed the bank with a kerchief on your
face. I vividly gave a description of this event under hypnosis,
your going into the Bank, your leaving the Bank. The details
can be found in Medical files, FBI files.) I called you on
cheating the elder Mr. Evans. You were irrate. Several days
later your sons, Richard and Don Jr. paid me an 8:00 p.m. visit
at your office, I was working an Aetna Survey on a commercial
account. Assuming their visit was friendly, I let them in,
sat back in the desk chair, as they railed about my telling
you how to pay off Mr. Evans etc., they jumped over the desk
top pushed me to the floor. I calmly restrained Richard as
Don Jr. ran to the bathroom, broke a coke bottle in half, as
he came at me I restrained him to the floor, till they both
began to cry.

-5-

EYHIRIT P

190

Little did I know when I left your agency that you, your peers would blacklist my character and career from San Luis Obispo to Wichita, KA to San Jose, CA. In San Jose, CA I found myself in trouble with the Mafia, Law Enforcement agents. At this point in time I'm no longer in trouble with the mafia or Law Enforcement agents. You, your peers utilized Retail Credit Co. under the then mgmt. of James H. Strowbridge, a vicious man, corrupt, took payoffs to cover adverse medical data or to blacklist a persons career. This ass often boasted how he would keep me broke, out of business, we will drive you insane, you will never get ahead in this country. There are twenty more pages to brief notes from my autobiography which I haven't time to disclose. In Santa Clara Valley you minipulated along with your peers, heaps of trouble, grief on me, directly infectious to my family current to date. In the Personal injury case of (1976) DiAnelli vs Mr. Myers my San Francisco, CA attorney advised me that I best move to W. Germany or Western Europe that your father, step father what ever he is and his attorney have me backlisted and I cannot give a fair settlement, we are going have to take a $5400 deficit. To this day I have no teeth. I have gone without teeth since 1976. accepting the daily pain.

It is interesting, I pressed my mind and spirit through 10,480 hours of mental gymnastic, raying, holding a firm Image of myself healed, consuming thousands of vitamins, on June 22, 1977 I began walking, my son Kevin had to come and pick me up. I kept walking untill I could fast walk 166 strides per minute, now I run, I'm a novdic style skiier. Sleeping with recordings on Positive thinking, meditating on Positive concepts, I learned to believe in myself, to Trust in God. Certain that this recovery was complete I married to began a new life.

Desiring to have a good life I research books on the mind, on rejection, on why some succeed, some fail, and never recover, I by telephone consulted with Professors at Harvard University, Yale, Cornell University Pennsylvania, Stanford. My son, Kevin fed me encouragement, attending Los Gatos Christian Church restored by confidence in Christ Jesus. Visualizing this new Paul, fervent prayer broke the fetters from my mind, encouragement from Federal Agents helped me gain self respect, phone visits with Alex Madonna fed my interest in following through. Alex once said slap your face, run cold water over your wrists, hands, bath your face, keep on going. Marvin Richard in 1978 gave me Matt 6;33 as a valuable scripture to dwell on. An F.B.I. agent handling the file on me made it clear you deserve a Gold medal. The Presidents High Ideals in his rigerous efforts to run the nation competently rallied my spirit. I pressed through tears, vomiting, tossing nights to enjoy a good life, a smooth spirit. One hundred eight hours of applied Hypnosis between two PhD, one in Los Altos, Ca, one in San Diego, CA.

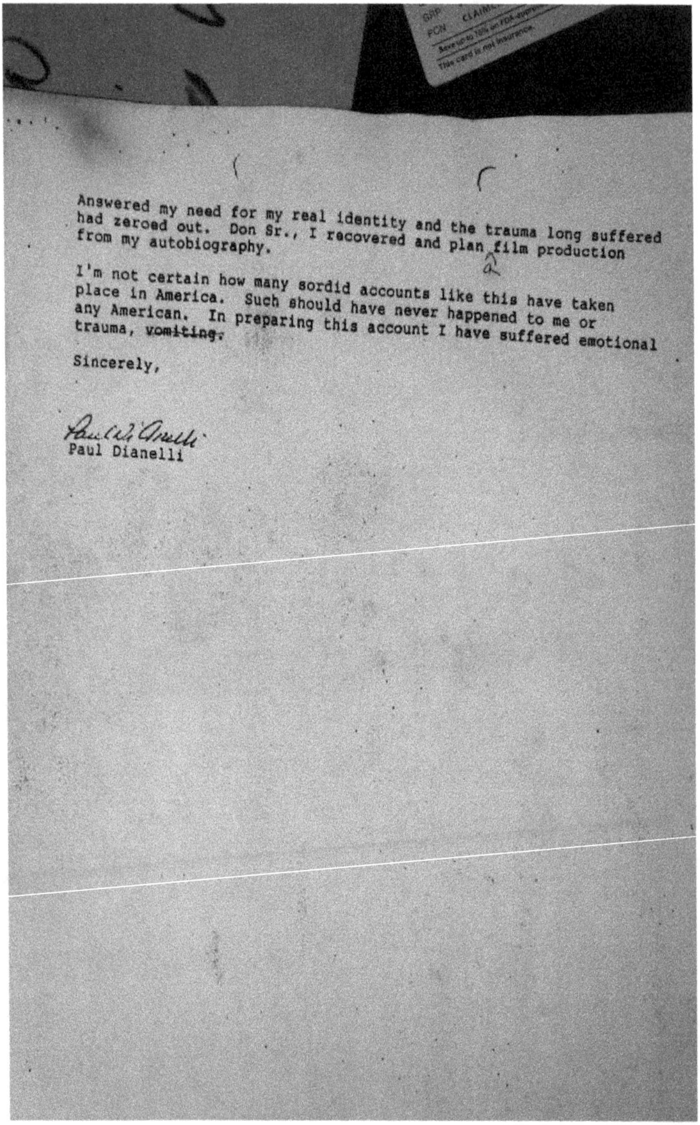

Answered my need for my real identity and the trauma long suffered
had zeroed out. Don Sr., I recovered and plan film production
from my autobiography.

I'm not certain how many sordid accounts like this have taken
place in America. Such should have never happened to me or
any American. In preparing this account I have suffered emotional
trauma, vomiting.

Sincerely,

Paul Dianelli

KEVIN HUSTED, SR.

POST THOUGHTS

CHARLES A. LINDBERGH JR.

June 22, 1930 - February 14, 2016

Charles A Lindbergh Jr.

This is where my story ends. Times have never been easy, and I have often wondered if I were crazy. However, I know I am not. My life, by all accounts, has not been normal, and there has been much interference

193

in me being able to establish myself as the son of Charles A. Lindbergh, Sr., and Anne Morrow Lindbergh. I know in my heart that I am their son and that I have siblings.

I have had many roadblocks and years of suffering. The only thing I ever wanted was to find my family and be accepted.

As I age, I grow weary, and my heart breaks for my children and their legacy. I guess life is never fair. I only want the truth to be told by all of those involved.

I voluntarily submitted to a polygraph test, which the examiner said I was telling the truth about my identity and submitted my DNA to no avail to prove my identity.

To me, I had everything to lose by doing so because it is my reputation that was on the line. I ask, "Why would I claim such a thing my entire life and take a chance on being proven a fraud?" Would you take such a risk?

I hired lawyers to help me uncover the truth and have had documentary filmmakers take interest in my story. However, none of this came to fruition as roadblock after roadblock surfaced.

Unfortunately, most of the people involved in this case are dead and cannot collaborate anything that I have said or refuse to discuss anything with me. I can't even get a simple answer from the FBI and the files they have. They claim it would go against other cases. I filed under the Freedom of Information Act, but most of the information is not fruitful as it is blackened out. I am at a loss.

To Charles A. Lindbergh Sr., and Anne Morrow Lindbergh, whom I believe are my parents, I have no words that can express the grief and sorrow in my heart. All I can say is you must have had a very good reason for not wanting to discover my true identity as your son. I felt deserted for years and always questioned when I saw you from across the street or from across the room, what I did to deserve this treatment. I did nothing to you. I honestly can say, that I have deep-boned grief for what could have been, and one day in Heaven, I will get my answer.

To my Lindbergh siblings, I believe that you are, although you don't. I will go to my grave in forgiveness. I remember so much of the pain and the suffering and the denials by the FBI and those involved in raising me who know the truth. Most of all, I remember growing up without you. I pray that you may one day find it in your heart to come forward with the truth.

I am not here to lambast anyone, especially the Lindbergh family. They will have to live with their decisions as I have had to. I will probably go to my grave, never being accepted in my destiny, but I pray that one day, somewhere, someone steps forward and has the courage to speak up about the truth and change history.

I remain sincerely,

Charles A. Lindbergh, Jr.

I REMEMBER

THE LINDBERGH CONSPIRACY BLOG

Thank you for reading this memoir of my father, Charles A. Lindbergh Jr. After his death, as his son, I inherited all of his notes, journals, and diaries. I chose to release them to the public to see if anyone could help us. For the purpose of uncovering the truth, I have created a blog called *The Lindbergh Baby Conspiracy* with the URL of:

https://lindberghbabyconspiracy.blogspot.com/

If you have any comments or information that can support what my father says, please go to the blog and leave your comments. You can also contact me there.

I remain,

Kevin Husted, Sr.

KEVIN HUSTED, SR.

www.ingramcontent.com/pod-product-compliance
Lightning Source LLC
Chambersburg PA
CBHW050114280326
41933CB00010B/1091